SO DEEPLY SCARRED

BY HOWARD MORGAN

Copyright © 2017 by Howard Morgan Ministries

All rights reserved. This book or any portion thereof may not be reproduced or used in any manner whatsoever without the express written permission of the publisher except for the use of brief quotations in a book review or scholarly journal.

First Printing: 2017

ISBN 978-1-329-06545-1

Edited by Susan Gaines, Camille Montgomery, Michael Senger, Susan Ohman and June Volk.

Cover art image *The Great Lament* by Bronislaw Linke used by permission from VirtualJudaica.com.

Cover art created by Melanie Morgan and Michael Senger

www.howardmorganministries.com

ENDORSEMENTS

Dr. Howard Morgan's *So Deeply Scarred* is a thoroughly researched, comprehensive study of the tragedy of historical antisemitism that also discusses Christian complicity in the unrelenting hatred, violence, and mayhem that have been directed toward the Jewish people for more than two millennia. This work is a must read for all Christians who are serious about following the teachings of Jesus - in this case, loving and supporting the Jewish family of their incarnate Lord.

John D. Garr, Ph.D.
Founder & President
Hebraic Christian Global Community
Founder and Senior Editor of Restore! Magazine

Dr. Howard Morgan has done God's people a great service by putting together a clear and concise summary of anti-Semitism in Church history. And as with all his teachings, his purpose is redemptive, not accusatory, since he recognizes the great calling on Gentile believers to provoke the Jewish people to envy, and in this important mini-book, he calls on the Church to distant itself from its anti-Semitic past and to rise up in the love and power of the Spirit.

Dr. Michael L. Brown,
Author, *Our Hands Are Stained with Blood: The Tragic Story of the "Church" and the Jewish People*

Having written a thing or two and knowing how much we sometimes have to research to be sure of the accuracy of even one sentence, I am stunned at the amount of clear information Howard has given us in this power-packed book. Anyone who will read the book with an open heart and mind will be moved to what is called "Identificational repentance and confession," as Daniel did so long ago, "O Lord have mercy. Forgive us for all that we have done against your covenant people in the past and are still doing. O Lord, change the hearts of your people who, even today, have turned against your people Israel!"

Don Finto
Pastor Emeritus Belmont Church Nashville, TN
Founder & Director of the Caleb Company
Author of God's Promise and the Future of Israel, Your People Shall Be My People, and, Prepare! For the End Time Harvest

So Deeply Scarred uncovers the history of satan's plan to annihilate the Jewish people off the face of the earth. Howard goes through the history of ant-Semitism and discloses how the European Church joined in with satan's plan of annihilation. So Deeply Scarred is timely, revealing the implications of Resolution 2234 passed by the United Nations on December 23, 2016, declaring Jewish existence in Jerusalem, Judea and Samaria as being 'illegal'. How does one respond concerning Israel, the Jewish people and one's faith in the Jewish Messiah, who is the Son of God? This book is riveting, a historical classic on anti-Semitism. A must read!

Shelly and June Volk
International Messianic Jewish ministers/authors

DEDICATION

May this book bring understanding to those authentic disciples of the Kingdom of God who are willing to learn the lessons of history and participate in God's plan for the restoration of the Body of Christ to her Biblical relationship and responsibility to the Jewish people. My prayer is that you become one of God's *"servants who find pleasure in Zion's stones and feel pity for her dust"* (Psalm 102:14) and in doing so, fulfill your destiny in God's end-time plan to *"Build up Zion and then appear in His Glory!"* (Psalm 102:16).

ACKNOWLEDGEMENTS

There is no greater gift of love that God can give to man than to have a wife who walks with him. Janet, my beloved, may God always *Shine His Face* on you!

To Dr. Jennifer Scrivner, a true lover of Zion, for her input into the very first draft and to Dr. John Garr, for his excellent editorial advice and most valuable friendship. To Camille Montgomery, June Volk, and Susan Ohman, for their many valuable suggestions and corrections. To Susan Gaines, my professional editor and good friend, who did what all good editors and friends do. May all your labors bear much fruit for the Kingdom of God!

TABLE OF CONTENTS

ENDORSEMENTS i
DEDICATION iii
ACKNOWLEDGEMENTS iv
TABLE OF CONTENTS v
PART I 1
   The Jews and the Return of Jesus 1
   The History of "Christian" Anti-Semitism 3
   Witnessing to the Jewish People 8
PART 2 13
   An Outline of the History of "Christian" Anti-Semitism 13
   Historical Periods 14
   The First 1000 Years 14
   The Crusades: 1000 - 1348 15
   The Black Death: 1348 - 1354 15
   The Inquisition: 1366-1500 16
   The Reformation: 1500 - 1599 18
   The 17th and 18th Centuries: 1600 - 1799 19
   The 19th Century: 1800 - 1899 20
      Russia 24
      France 25
      The Dreyfus Affair 25
      The Muslim World 26
   20th Century Anti-Semitism 26
      Russia 26
      Nazi Germany 27
      Latin America 27
      America 28
   21st Century Anti-Semitism 29
      The Islamic World 30

- Categories of Anti-Semitic Persecution 31
  - 1) Anti-Semitism Enacted into Law or State Policy 31
  - 2) Official Charges Lodged Against Jews 35
  - 3) Proselytizing Prohibited 41
  - 4) Confiscation of Property 42
  - 5) Destruction of Property 45
  - 6) Discrimination and Unjust Taxation 46
  - 7) Segregation 51
  - 8) Slander 54
  - 9) Mandatory Conversion 62
  - 10) Imprisonment, Torture and Slavery 65
  - 11) Murder and Slaughter of Individual Jews 66
  - 12) Execution of Parents and Separation of Children from Parents 69
  - 13) Mob Attacks and Riots 71
  - 14) Jewish Communities and Quarters Attacked and Burned 74
  - 15) Wearing of Badges or Distinctive Dress to Identify Jews 77
  - 16) Expulsion of Jews 78
  - 17) Mass Extermination of Jews 80
- Instances of Aid to the Jews 84
- The Holocaust 1933-1945 90
  - Holocaust Statistics 91
- A Selected Overview of Holocaust Events 94
- 21st Century Anti-Semitism 103
  - Anti-Semitism Continues to the Present Day 103
- Resources for Further Study 106
  - Anti-Semitism 106
  - Holocaust Studies 107

SO DEEPLY SCARRED

PART I

The Jews and the Return of Jesus

From the beginning of human history, Satan has sought to prevent the plans and purposes of God from being fulfilled. He knows that the Jewish people are a central part of the plan of God for the redemption of the world. He knows that the regathering of the Jewish people to the land of Israel is a fulfillment of prophecy and a necessary precursor to the return of Jesus. He also knows that the restoration of the Church to her Biblical relationship and responsibility to the Jewish people is an important part of the process of reconciling the Jews to Jesus. Satan knows that the Scriptures teach that when the Jews receive Yeshua (Jesus) as their Messiah, it will mean the return of Jesus, the resurrection of the dead, the establishment of the Messianic Kingdom on the earth and his ultimate eternal damnation.[1] This is why he rigorously and ruthlessly tries to prevent this from happening by trying to destroy the Jewish people.

In Acts 3:21, the Apostle Peter declared that Jesus must remain in heaven *"until the times of the restoration of all things, which God hath spoken by the mouth of all His holy prophets since the world began."* Satan understands that if Jesus is being kept in heaven until the words of the prophets are fulfilled, then all he has to do to prevent the return of Jesus is stop the words of the prophets from being fulfilled. He knows what the prophets have said. He knows the Covenantal promises of God to the Jewish people. He knows that God scattered the Jewish people to the nations of the world as a punishment for their disobedience.[2] He also knows that God declared that they would never be destroyed, and that God would, at the end of the age, have mercy on them and regather them to their ancient homeland and send their Messianic King Jesus to rule and reign over the nations from Jerusalem.[3]

---

[1] Romans 11:15; 1 Thessalonians 4:15; Revelation 20:4, 10
[2] Leviticus 26:33; Deuteronomy 28:64
[3] Jeremiah 30:9; Hosea 3:5; Ezekiel 34:23, 37:24; Psalm 2:6-9; Zechariah 14:3,4; Revelation 20:4,6

Knowing all this, Satan developed a twofold plan to try to prevent the return of Jesus. The first part of this plan was to try to stop the words of the prophets from being fulfilled by either killing the Jewish people or causing them to be assimilated into the nations of the world and lose their national distinctiveness. In this way, when God's *"time to have mercy on Zion"*[4] would arrive, He would not find any Jewish people to regather. They would have either all been killed, or so assimilated into the various cultures of the world that there would be no one who would identify themselves as Jews.

The second part of Satan's plan focused on the Church. By convincing the Church to arrogantly reject her Jewish roots and the Jewish people, the Church was *"cut off from the rich root of the Olive Tree"*[5] and was replanted into the soil of Greco-Roman humanistic, pagan beliefs and practices. These influences so perverted the Church, that she developed a new non-biblical *religion* that deceptively called itself *Christianity*.

Under Satan's influence this *Christian religion* became an instrument of hatred and death that ruthlessly persecuted the Jewish people in the name of Jesus. **Instead of provoking the Jews to life-transforming faith in Jesus, the Church provoked the Jews to *despise* even the mention of His name!** Jesus said to the Jewish people that they would not see Him again until they said to Him, *"Blessed is He who comes in the name of the Lord."*[6] What will inspire the Jewish people to say that? God's plan is to have a people who are so filled with the love and power of the Holy Spirit that they would be able to provoke natural Israel to spiritual jealousy.[7] Even if the Jews reject that witness (how often have I heard, "I'm so glad that works for you, but I am a Jew"), God will use that testimony when He pours out the *"Spirit of grace and of supplication"*[8] upon the Jewish people. Then the magnificent age-ending revelation of who Jesus really is will break forth upon them

---

[4] Psalm 102:13
[5] Romans 11:18-22
[6] Matthew 23:39
[7] Deuteronomy 32:21; Romans 11:11,14
[8] Zechariah 12:10

and they *"will look on (Him) whom they have pierced; and they will mourn for Him as one mourns for an only son."*[9] On that day of national repentance, they will call out to Yeshua (Jesus) to come and save them. He will return, raise the dead and establish His Kingdom on the earth!!

The History of "Christian" Anti-Semitism

Our study of the history of the Church and the Jewish people reveals a devastatingly clear and undeniable revelation of one of the most fundamental Christian heresies: "Christian" Anti-Semitism. We confront a paradox. There can be no such thing as "Christian" Anti-Semitism; for Anti-Semitism is not only fundamentally unchristian, it is actually Anti-Christian. Yet Anti-Semitism flows throughout history as one of the most enduring characteristics of many of those who claimed to be followers of Christ. Unless we understand this reality, we will not be able to confront it and rise above it. Unless we rise above it, we will have no spiritual authority to be Godly witnesses of Jesus to the Jews. For how can we claim to love Jesus and not have His love for His own people?[10]

The history of "Christian" Anti-Semitism is a history of hatred. It is arguably the most persistent and violent hatred that has plagued human history. It was aptly summed up by the French Jewish scholar, Jules Isaac, who described it as the "teaching of contempt for the Jews."[11] To understand this history we must learn about the great corruption that entered into the *spiritual* life of the Church as it became a *religious/political* institution that was a *counterfeit* of the authentic Body of Christ. We can then see how Anti-Semitism was manifested in beliefs and actions that led to nearly twenty centuries of humiliation, rejection, disgrace, degradation, isolation, persecution, expulsions, pogroms (government sponsored massacres) and ultimately genocide.

---

[9] Ibid
[10] Matthew 23:37; Romans 9:2
[11] Isaac, Jules. *The Teaching of Contempt*, McGraw-Hill, 1965.

As we study "Christian" Anti-Semitism, we will discover the specific reasons for the following description of the escalation of Anti-Semitism throughout the ages. As the Church grew in political, financial and military power it sought to forcibly convert Jews to its version of *Christianity*. Holocaust scholar Raul Hilberg, in his book *The Destruction of the European Jews*, encapsulated the edicts of the Church toward the Jewish people. First, they were told, "**You have no right to live among us as Jews.**" As the Jews resisted this perse-cution and held onto the Torah and their religious beliefs and traditions, this spiritually corrupted politicized counterfeit "Church" said to the Jews, "**You have no right to live among us.**" This created urban ghettos, separate rural areas of settlement and even total national expulsions. These Anti-Semitic beliefs created the cultural, spiritual and religious foundations for the Nazis who said, "**You have no right to live.**"

Following Hilberg, we can summarize the historical progression of "Christian" Anti-Semitism in this way:
1. **You have no right to live among us as Jews.**
2. **You have no right to live among us.**
3. **You have no right to live.**

In this book, I have organized this history chronologically. It shows a pattern repeated again and again from the Roman period through the present day. We witness Crusades, Inquisitions, Expulsions and Pogroms, all of which culminated in the Holocaust. As we study this history we can see the year-by-year, decade-by-decade and century-by-century operation of the spirit of Anti-Semitism. History shows us when, where and how it spread. It temporarily subsides in one place and then emerges in another. We are witnessing its present-day resurgence, not only via violent terrorist attacks but in many other ways as well.

The unthinkable horror of the Holocaust was the bitter fruit of long centuries of false teaching about the Jewish people. Beginning with the early Gentile Church fathers (who were influenced by Greek/Hellenic philosophy), anti-Jewish doctrines began to be institutionalized when the Roman emperor Constantine established *Christianity* as the religion of the empire. Ironically the Church that was

PART I – THE HISTORY OF "CHRISTIAN" ANTI-SEMITISM

once persecuted by *triumphant* and *imperialistic* Roman emperors adapted those very same philosophies. Seeing themselves as the *Church triumphant*, they began to exercise their newfound political power in worldly and not Kingdom ways. This Hellenized Roman "Christianity" treated the Jewish people with contempt. Rejecting the Apostle Paul's admonition, Church leaders arrogantly rejected the *"branches"* they were grafted into and the very root that nourished them.[12] The result was that the apostle's prophetic warning came to pass. The Church was *"cut off"*[13] and as history shows us, descended into centuries of spiritual darkness.

The extent of Anti-Semitism in Church history is not typically taught in most churches, Bible schools or seminaries. Today there is a tendency to assume that the problem of Jewish security and the attitudes of Jews toward their survival grows from the experience of the Holocaust alone. The unspeakable crimes of the Nazis and their collaborators are so high on the scale of horror that they tend to eclipse the long history of Anti-Semitism. Many people do not understand that the underlying forces that created the Holocaust are almost 2,000 years old. The genocide carried out by a supposed *civilized* and *cultured* Germany in the mid-20th century was an extreme, but not isolated, manifestation of this ancient spirit.

Auschwitz Gate

Throughout its history, the Church has been influenced by *"deceitful spirits and doctrines of demons"*[14] that have perverted her relationship with the Jewish people. Obeying these demonic forces, the Church wielded an evil sword of hatred, persecution and murder against the Jews. This demonically deceived religion was so far from what the Bible teaches that it was easy for its merely

---

[12] Romans 11:18
[13] Romans 11:22
[14] 1 Timothy 4:1

"Christianized" members to follow their ungodly leaders on paths of hatred, persecution and murder.

Because these leaders were not under the influence of the Holy Spirit and did not obey the clear teachings of the New Testament, they usurped the authentic spiritual authority of the Body of Christ using it for their own worldly financial, political and military goals. Instead of using their spiritual authority to make and mature fruitful disciples of the Kingdom of God, they turned the Church into their own *empire*. Then, like any other worldly empire, they intimidated, manipulated and controlled their followers; persecuting or killing those whom they perceived to be a threat to their power and authority, including authentic believers.

This is the exact opposite of Jesus' instructions to those who would become leaders in His Church. In all three synoptic Gospels, Jesus commands them *"not to be like the Gentiles, who rule over others, but instead be their servants."*[15] The authentic Body of Christ does not persecute anyone.[16] True Christians know that they can never coerce or force anyone to come to faith in Jesus. That is a supernatural work of the Holy Spirit.[17] Therefore they leave the results of evangelism to God. Jesus also taught that His disciples are to love everyone, even those who reject them.[18] They are never to take vengeance on anyone.[19] This shows us how very far from the Lordship of Jesus and being an authentic expression of the Kingdom of God that this counterfeit persecutorial Church had gone.

The Jews were considered a threat. The Scriptures were entrusted to them.[20] They had a long religious history with their own understanding and traditional interpretations of the Bible. Their rejection of Jesus and resistance to the Church's authority would naturally provoke people to ask, "If Yeshua (Jesus) is the Jewish

---

[15] Matthew 20:25; Mark 10:42; Luke 22:25
[16] 1 John 3:10-15
[17] John 6:44,65
[18] Matthew 5:43-46
[19] Deuteronomy 32:35; Romans 12:19
[20] Romans 3:2

PART I – THE HISTORY OF "CHRISTIAN" ANTI-SEMITISM

Messiah, why don't the Jews believe in him? Maybe he is not really the Messiah and the Church is wrong." This kind of thinking was a serious threat to those insecure, carnal and worldly Church leaders.

In seeking to minimize any possible influence from the Jewish community, those paranoid leaders sought to instill in the Church a fear of the Jewish people. Christians were forbidden from having anything to do with the Jews or their religious practices or beliefs. The Jewish people were vilified in sermons and castigated from pulpits as, among other lies and distortions, *Christ-Killers* who deserve to be punished for that crime.[21] This continual demonization of the Jewish people eventually bred enough hatred for the Jews that to persecute and kill the *evil* Jews became *reasonable* and "Christian."

God's plan was, and still is, to use Israel's rejection of Jesus as the way to open the doors of salvation to the nations. Believing Gentiles who are *"grafted in,"*[22] *"saved"*[23] and members of the *"Commonwealth of Israel"*[24] are called to extend a loving hand bearing the fruits and gifts of their salvation to the Jewish people. This testimony of love and faith in action, including miraculous demonstrations of the power of the Holy Spirit,[25] is intended to *"provoke the Jews to jealousy"*[26] and cause them to see that the rejected Jesus is in fact their long awaited Messiah.

Listening to, believing and acting on the clever lies of the devil, who is the *"father of lies,"*[27] the Church rejected the *"natural branches"* of the *"Olive Tree"* and became infected with spirits of Anti-Semitism. When she rejected the *"anointed roots"* of the *"Olive*

---

[21] Although some Jewish leaders were partially responsibility for the death of Jesus, it was God's eternal plan (1 Peter 1:20; Revelation 13:8). All Jews everywhere throughout history are not guilty of "killing Jesus" – who willingly died for their sins and yours.
[22] Romans 11:17
[23] Ephesians 2:5,8
[24] Ephesians 2:12-19
[25] Acts 4:33; 1 Corinthians 2:5, 4:20; Galatians 3:5; Hebrews 2:4
[26] Romans 11:11
[27] John 8:44

Tree," she rejected the ministry of the Holy Spirit[28] and was infected with "*Spirits of Religion.*" They corrupted the Church with many demonic doctrines, all intended to create a new *non-Biblical counterfeit religion* that did not make, nor mature, authentic fruitful disciples of the Kingdom. These two demonic principalities, *Anti-Semitism* and *Religion*, combined to create a *Christianity* that did two things – persecute the Jews in order to keep them from Jesus and thereby hinder His return, and keep the people from becoming authentic maturing fruitful disciples. How cleverly wicked is this twofold plan! Keep the Church carnal, Biblically ignorant, spiritually weak and worldly. Keep the Jews from Jesus and try to prevent His return.

Witnessing to the Jewish People

As modern day followers of Jesus, we must learn the truth about Christianity's relationship with the Jewish people because it is part of our history as Christians. We must know the truth about those who proclaimed themselves to be the representatives of the Lord Jesus. We cannot separate ourselves from our spiritual ancestors, whether they were true Christians or not. Because our spiritual ancestors persecuted the Jewish people in the name of Jesus and claimed to represent Him and His Church, we have a responsibility to acknowledge their sins and crimes and renounce and reject their Anti-Semitism. This is absolutely foundational for any believer who wants to be an effective witness to the Jewish people.

One reason this is so necessary is that to the majority of Jewish people today there is an historic connection between those who claimed to be "Christians" and persecuted them, and modern "Christians," whom many Jews believe are only motivated to *convert* them to Christianity. For the Jewish person, *conversion* does not have the Biblical meaning of a spiritual rebirth,[29] the forgiveness of sins[30] and the creation of a new personal relationship

---

[28] Romans 11:17-24
[29] John 3:3-8
[30] Luke 24:47; Acts 2:38, 5:31, 10:43; Colossians 1:13-14

PART I – THE HISTORY OF "CHRISTIAN" ANTI-SEMITISM

with the God of Israel.[31] To the majority of Jews, the word *conversion* means rejecting and abandoning their family, people, heritage, traditions, culture and religion. Simply put, conversion means becoming a *non-Jew*.

As we remorsefully recognize the sinful history of Anti-Semitism, we will, by the power of the Holy Spirit, be able to develop Godly responses to its modern-day manifestations and use that as a part of developing a credible testimony to the Jewish people of lives changed by their Messiah. This will also reflect the very heart of Jesus who wept over Jerusalem,[32] and the Apostle Paul, who carried a *"great sorrow and continual grief"*[33] for his own beloved Jewish people.

As you understand the history of "Christian" Anti-Semitism, you will recognize the demonic forces that resist the witness of your faith in Jesus to a Jewish person. Please understand that I am speaking in generalities. In this, as in all areas of human activity, there are individual differences. Throughout history, Jewish people have come to faith in Jesus as there has always been a believing remnant.[34] However, you will find the vast majority of Jewish people are closed to the Gospel. Learning this horrific history will help you understand their rejection of Jesus as their Messiah.

Because of centuries of oppression and persecution by the Church in the name of Jesus, the Jewish people have been enfolded in a spiritual realm that resists the Gospel. This persecution by the Church has only reinforced the spiritual blindness to the Gospel that God Himself has put upon the Jewish people.[35] This blindness is only *"in part"*[36] and it is only in reference to the Messiahship of Jesus, so that Gentiles can experience *"salvation and the spiritual riches of the Gospel."*[37] Obey the apostle's admonition to *"not get*

---

[31] Jeremiah 9:23-24; John 17:3; Philippians 3:8-14
[32] Matthew 23:37
[33] Romans 9:1-3
[34] Romans 9:27, 11:4-5
[35] Romans 11:7-10
[36] Romans 11:25
[37] Romans 11:11-12, 25

arrogant in your heart"[38] and think that the Jewish people are completely spiritually blind; they are not. There are many wonderful truths and spiritual insights available to you within the vast treasure of Jewish learning.

Within the spiritual realm accompanying Jewish evangelism there is much unforgiveness on the part of the Jewish people towards the historic Christian Church. Jesus taught us that if we want to be forgiven, we must forgive.[39] This applies to the Jews as well as everyone else. Until a Jewish person forgives the Church for its sins, unforgiveness will infect their heart. This infection creates all manner of spiritual bitterness which hardens the heart towards God (who allows all of this when He has the power to stop it) and of course, to Jesus and or the apostle Paul (who are seen as the founders of the religion that hates the Jews). In various times and places we see Jewish unforgiveness manifesting itself by cursing Jesus and His Church. In classic polemical fashion, for example, some rabbis even distorted the name of Yeshua and made it Yeshu, which is an acronym for "Yemach Shemo Verzichro" *may his name and memory be blotted out*, or alternately *may his name be obliterated and forgotten.* Similarly they turned the Greek word for Gospel, Good-News, "Evangelion" into the Hebrew words "Avon Gilion" which means "The Scroll of Sin." From a merely human perspective it is easy to understand these responses to persecution. Nevertheless, unforgiveness is a sin that opens anyone to the maleficent influences and nefarious activities of demons.[40]

As you read this history be aware that your spirit may be grieved. You may weep as you read. You may have the same experience I did when I wrote this book. I could hear in my spirit the blood-curdling screams of these victims. I could hear the gut wrenching cries of the parents and their children as panic, fear and pain overwhelmed them. All of this perpetrated by those who called themselves "Christians," and who declared that it was "Jesus Christ" who commanded them to inflict this great suffering and pain upon

---

[38] Romans 11:18
[39] Matthew 6:14-15
[40] 2 Corinthians 2:10-11

PART I – THE HISTORY OF "CHRISTIAN" ANTI-SEMITISM

the Jews. In the face of such horrific onslaughts, how could the Jewish people possibly believe that "He" was their long hoped for Messiah?

God says that *"the voice of Abel's blood cries to Him from the ground."*[41] I believe that this does not just refer to Abel's blood, but to all the innocent blood that has ever been shed. The Book of Revelation also reveals to us that the blood of those martyred for the Gospel also cries out to God.[42] I take great comfort in the fact that the Blood of Jesus speaks *"better things"* than the blood of Abel.[43] These *"better things"* are the salvation and ultimate redemption that God will bring upon the entire earth. He promises us that one day **"the whole earth will be filled with the knowledge of the glory of God, as the waters cover the sea."**[44]

I understand that reading about this history of persecution and death is very difficult. It was very difficult for me to put this together. There were times when I had to stop the research because it was too painful. The woman who originally typed the history for me had times when she had to stop and cry because she was so shocked, having never heard that all this evil had been perpetrated in the name of Jesus. I said to her, "I believe that you represent many people who just don't know about these things, and will have the same reaction as you."

If you want to share the Gospel with Jewish people, you need to know this history of persecution and death. It will explain to you why the name of *Jesus* or why the words like *New Testament, Christian, Christ* or *Cross,* or images of it, cause such a strong negative reaction from Jewish people. They are still **"*So Deeply Scarred*."**

---

[41] Genesis 4:10
[42] Revelation 6:9-10
[43] Hebrews 12:22-24
[44] Isaiah 11:9; Habakkuk 2:14

SO DEEPLY SCARRED

A depiction of the Church rejecting and persecuting the Jewish people.

PART 2

An Outline of the History of "Christian" Anti-Semitism

In my original research for this book I had about 350 printed pages of Anti-Semitic incidents. I present here only about one tenth of them to give you a picture of this history. In order to condense the information, I have attempted to analyze all of the incidents and put them into 17 different categories. The 1900 years was divided into six different historical periods, during which persecution in these 17 different categories *actually took place*.[45]

Historical periods:
1) The First 1000 Years.
2) The Crusades.
3) The Black Death.
4) The Inquisition.
5) The Reformation.
6) The 17th and 18th Centuries.
7) The 19th Century.
8) The 20th Century.
9) The 21st Century.

Categories:
1) Anti-Semitism Enacted into the Law and made into State Policy.
2) Official Charges against Jews.
   a) Deicide.
   b) Ritual Murder.
   c) Well Poisoning.
   d) Host Desecration.
3) Proselytizing Prohibited.
4) Confiscation of Property.
5) Destruction of Property.

---

[45] This outline is based on "Anti-Semitism: Causes and Effects" by Paul Grosser and Edwin Halperin, 1983, Philosophical Library.

6) Discrimination and Unjust Taxation.
7) Segregation.
8) Slander.
9) Mandatory Conversion (Suicide Preferred to Conversion).
10) Imprisonment, Torture, Sold into Slavery.
11) Murder and Slaughter of Individual Jews.
12) Execution of Parents and Separation of Children from Parents.
13) Mob Riots and Attacks.
14) Jewish Communities or Quarters Attacked and Burned.
15) Wearing of Badges or Distinctive Dress to Identify the Jews.
16) Expulsions.
17) Mass Exterminations.

Instances of Aid to the Jews p. 84

The Holocaust 1933-1945 p. 90

21st Century Anti-Semitism p. 103

Historical Periods

An overview of the history of Anti-Semitism will show us that the ancient Greeks and Romans possessed an Anti-Semitism that was focused on ethnic differences. Christian and Muslim Anti-Semitism was religious in nature. After the Enlightenment in Europe, Anti-Semitism was political, social and economic. This laid the groundwork for the racial Anti-Semitism of the 19th and early 20th century that culminated in the Holocaust. Modern Anti-Semitism is fueled by radical fundamentalist Islam's focus on destroying Israel.

The First 1000 Years

After Christianity became the *official* religion of Rome in the 4th century, Anti-Semitism was manifested in various ways. Jews were victims of religious and political persecution. Beginning with

PART 2 – AN OUTLINE OF THE HISTORY OF "CHRISTIAN" ANTI-SEMITISM

Constantine and the council of Nicaea, edicts from Church councils resulted in various forms of discrimination and religious oppression. Christians were forbidden from celebrating the Passover, keeping the Jewish Sabbath or converting to Judaism. This discrimination included barring Jews from participation in various social and economic activities and being relegated to second class status.

The Crusades: 1000 - 1348

The Middle Ages was a time when ignorance, cruelty and superstition reigned. As non-Christians in Europe, during an age when the explanation for everything negative was the devil, the Jews (as the *Christ rejecter* and accused as the *Christ-Killer*) were believed to be Satan's emissaries. This engendered a fear of and hatred for the Jewish people. This isolated the Jews and caused day-to-day repercussions in Jewish life which was an existence of total instability, insecurity and at times absolute terror. They regularly experienced attacks, slaughters, extortions, expulsions, kidnappings, forced baptism, confiscation of property, ridicule and humiliation.

The Crusades opened a new era of ferocious Anti-Semitism. In the 11th and 12th centuries, Anti-Semitic and Anti-Jewish doctrines and preaching inspired many atrocities. Civil and religious authorities were often in the role of restraining the masses and protecting the Jews from popular attack. Things got worse in the 13th century as restraints were lifted by Anti-Semitic leaders. Techniques of mass torture and slaughter were added to the former practices of forced baptism, expulsion, restriction and extortion.

The Black Death: 1348 - 1354

The *Black Death* period is extremely important to the history and development of Anti-Semitism. With thousands dying of the plague, the cause was ascribed to the Jews who were suspected of an international conspiracy aimed at the extermination of Christians. Jews were accused of poisoning wells thus causing the plague. They were also accused of killing Christian children and using their blood to make Matzo (unleavened bread) for the Passover Seder, which is referred to as *ritual murder*. They were further accused of *Host Desecration* (stealing and then repeatedly stabbing the *Host* used in the Catholic Mass).

Jews were victims of expulsions and unjust taxation. Their property was confiscated and they were restricted socially, economically and religiously. They suffered forced baptism, torture, plunder and mass slaughter.

A woodcut depicting the accusation of Jews killing a Christian child

The Inquisition: 1366-1500

The Inquisition was a Roman Catholic institution which focused on exposing and removing heretics. Established in 1480 in Toledo, Spain, the Catholic hierarchy sought to purify their Church of all Catholics whose beliefs and practices varied from their own brand of orthodoxy.

Under the leadership of the Dominican priest, Thomas de Torquemada, (who had Jewish ancestry), known as the *Grand Inquisitor*, the inquisition focused on finding and removing those Jews who outwardly converted to Catholicism, but secretly practiced

PART 2 – AN OUTLINE OF THE HISTORY OF "CHRISTIAN" ANTI-SEMITISM

Judaism, as well as those Jews who helped them maintain their Jewish identity and religious practice. Torquemada's reign lasted 16 years during which time he, and the pious sadists who served him, were responsible for burning approximately 2000 so called "heretics" and imprisoning and ruining the lives of tens of thousands of others.

From 1481 onwards, the Inquisition conducted a systematic war against the Jews who were known variously as Marranos (Swine), Conversos or New Christians, Crypto-Jews and Anusim (Coerced Converts). These people were subject to horrific agonizing forms of coercive torture to extract confessions of their Jewish practices. Often those who confessed were burned alive, in what was called an "Auto de Fe – Act of Faith." These public burnings were a warning to the general public to remain faithful and obedient to the Catholic Church.

Because many of these superficial converts found it socially, politically and economically beneficial to join the Catholic Church, the deeply religious Spanish Monarchs, King Ferdinand and Queen Isabella, considered these secret Jews to be a threat to the religious and social life of Spain. Their paranoia eventually led to the expulsion of all the Jews from Spain on July 31, 1492. Ironically, this date in the Jewish calendar was the Ninth of Av. On this very same day, many tragedies have befallen the Jewish people. On the Ninth of Av the first and second Temples were destroyed; the first by the Babylonians in 586 B.C.,

An Inquisition torture chamber
(Note the Priest and Crucifix)
(This is one reason why Jews hate the sign of the cross - wouldn't you?)

the second by the Romans in 70 A.D. The Jews were also expelled from England on this day in 1290.

The Reformation: 1500 - 1599

In 1543, Luther, who said this about the mistreatment of the Jews, "If it is a mark of a good Christian to hate the Jews, what excellent Christians all of us are," published *On the Jews and their Lies*. All students of history will recognize this book as being a blueprint for Adolf Hitler's genocidal program known as the final solution to the problem. In this book he describes the Jewish people in extremely harsh terms giving detailed directives for persecuting them.

Luther wrote:

> "Set their synagogues on fire, and whatever does not burn up should be covered or spread over with dirt so that not one man may ever be able to see a cinder or stone of it. Their homes should likewise be broken down and destroyed. They shall be put under one roof, or in a stable, like gypsies, in order that they may realize that they are not masters in our land, as they boast, but miserable captives, as they complain of us before God with bitter wailing. They should be deprived of their prayer books and Talmuds in which such idolatry, lies, cursing and blasphemy are taught. Their rabbis must be forbidden to teach under threat of death. We are at fault in not slaying them."

As part of his final sermon shortly before his death in 1546, Luther preached: "We want to treat the Jews with Christian love and to pray for them, so that they might become converted and would receive the Lord." However, as the sermon continued, he did continue his Anti-Semitic attacks.

During the period of the Reformation, instability, tension, along with political and religious ferment again found a handy scapegoat in the Jews. The standard techniques developed earlier were again used in attacking the Jews. Anti-Semitic practices of the time included:

- Forced Baptism
- Confiscation of property
- Expulsion
- Imprisonment
- Torture
- Execution
- Mob attacks (including arson, pillage and slaughter)
- Discriminatory taxation
- Burning of sacred writings
- Forced labor
- Prohibition of religious practice and proselytizing
- Restrictions on occupation, movement and residence
- Prescribed clothing
- Ritual Murder and Host Desecration charges

The 17th and 18th Centuries: 1600 - 1799

The 17th and 18th centuries were periods of decline in massive Anti-Semitic outbreaks in Western Europe, but there were a few incidents of outright slaughter. There were periodic expulsions, and the use of less violent techniques of Anti-Semitism was implemented. While the Inquisition in Spain and Portugal continued to persecute Marranos, the real tragedies occurred in Eastern Europe.

Jews had previously found protection and refuge in the East when fleeing persecution in Western Europe during the Crusades and the Inquisition, but now they were the victims of terrible persecutions and wholesale slaughter. Bogdan Khmelnytsky's Cossacks massacred tens of thousands of Jews in the eastern and southern areas that he controlled (now the Ukraine). The incredible atrocities of the Cossack and Tartar massacres were added to the tactics and techniques of the past: religious and civil restrictions which included discriminatory taxation, economic limitations, confiscation of money and property, expulsion, forced conversion, ritual murder charges, blasphemy charges, confiscation of holy writings and scapegoating.

The horrific Cossack massacres led many Jews to believe in Shabbatai Zevi who proclaimed himself Messiah in 1665. Under threat of death by the Ottoman Sultan, he converted to Islam.

This period did, however, have some positive aspects. In many Western European countries the *Age of Enlightenment* began to give new rights and freedoms to the Jewish people even though not all Enlightenment thinkers were positive toward the Jews. For example, Voltaire, one of the most influential individuals in France, had notorious Anti-Semitic views. Even so, the secularization of society that the *Enlightenment* started opened the doors for the Jews to assimilate and integrate into all levels of society. Modern Reformed Judaism was eventually birthed out of this dynamic.

As secularism and the democratic and scientific revolutions became the order of the day, it appeared that Anti-Semitism might be dying out in Western European tradition. For example, when Peter Stuyvesant, the Dutch leader of the colony of New Amsterdam, later New York City, sought to discriminate against the Jews there, he was removed from his post by his superiors.

The 19th Century: 1800 - 1899

Please note that Hitler was born in 1889 and like most Nazis, he grew up in a culture steeped in these Anti-Semitic beliefs. The Nazis took them to their "logical" conclusion.

The 19th century was one of considerable progress toward equality and full citizenship for Jews. This tendency was most evident in areas influenced by the Protestant Reformation and the Enlightenment. The persecution of Jews during this period was less systematic, less pervasive and not as constant as in previous centuries. Religious pluralism and the rise of religious tolerance in this increasingly secular age are generally given credit for the mildness and decline of persecution.

PART 2 – AN OUTLINE OF THE HISTORY OF "CHRISTIAN" ANTI-SEMITISM

Arising with this new found liberty and freedom for the Jewish people, came a demonic influence into the Church in Germany. So called "Enlightenment Rationalism" produced liberal Bible Scholars who created a school of theology known as "Higher Criticism" centered in Tübingen, Germany. Leaders like Friedrich Schleiermacher, David Strauss, Ludwig Feuerbach, Karl Graf and Julius Wellhausen, taught that the Bible was not Holy Scripture. It was not the authoritative and divinely inspired Word of God. They effecttively undermined the faith for much of the Church in Germany. This helped to create a spiritual vacuum into which various pagan, occult and anti-Christian belief systems, such as Theosophy and Ariosophy (which taught the myth of the "Aryan master race" and the need to "exterminate" lesser races in order to purify their blood), flourished. Inspired by occultists like Guido von List and Lanz von Liebenfels, these doctrines were Ultra-nationalistic and explicitly anti-Semitic. They were the spiritual breeding ground that enabled Nazi doctrines to infiltrate and overtake the entire German nation. It became a country of "cultured pagans" who, for example, could easily attend the Symphony one night and perpetrate horrific crimes of genocide the next day.

Ironically, Liberal Judaism was born during this same era. These liberal German Jewish leaders also rejected the supernatural origins and authority of their own Scriptures. They taught that real Jewish freedom would come only as Jews became "modern people." Believing that the highly cultured and intellectual German world was the best example of modernity, they became more "German" than "Jewish."

Despite the positive influences that began to ameliorate religious Anti-Semitism, a new, and what would become an even more virulent, form of Anti-Semitism began to emerge. It is called racial Anti-Semitism. This marked a shift in the focus of Anti-Jewish thinking. The religious factors were downplayed, and the emphasis became one of race and ideology. The racial theorist, Joseph Arthur de Gobineau, who was not personally Anti-Semitic, became famous for developing the theory of the Aryan master race in his book, *An Essay on the Inequality of the Human Race*, published in 1853. His ideology of race was based on the fiction that blonde European

"Aryans" had founded all major civilizations before being degraded by interbreeding with lesser racial groups.

In 1878, Rev. Dr. Adolph Stocker, Kaiser Wilhelm I's court preacher, founded the Christian Socialist Party. He coined the slogan which became a battle cry of the Nazis against the Jews: "Deutschland – erwache!" (Germany – awake!). He declared that "modern Judaism is an alien drop of blood in the German body – one with destructive power" and called for a Germany which would be Judenrein (free of Jews).

In 1879, the term *Anti-Semite* was coined by Wilhelm Marr. His book, *The Victory of Judaism over the Germans* set forth the major points of modern Anti-Semitism. He did not attack Judaism, declaring that it was idiotic to blame the Jews for the crucifixion. Marr did believe in defending the Jews against all religious persecution. He did recognize the abilities of the Jewish people who were economically and legally restricted. He did, however, see the Jews as a negative influence upon the German people. He accused the Jews of corrupting moral standards and dominating commerce, the theater and the press. He warned against hating individual Jews and upheld the belief that the Jewish people, as a race, were a very determined people who could not be changed.

Hermann Ahlwardt's three-volume work, *The Desperate Struggle of the Aryan Peoples with Judaism,* published from 1890 - 1892 had a major influence on Nazi Anti-Semitism. In it he depicted the Jews as a monstrous "octopus" controlling every phase of German life: the army, government, business, education and agriculture. The Jews were accused of a conspiracy to assassinate the Kaiser in 1878. The Jews were accused of financially enslaving the ruling class and exploiting and undermining Germany's economic health and stability. He publicly proclaimed that the Jews were *predators* and *cholera bacilli* who should be *exterminated* for the good of the German people.

Houston Stewart Chamberlain published *The Foundations of the Nineteenth Century* in 1899. This is perhaps the most libelous book ever written about the Jewish people. It won the acclaim and support

PART 2 – AN OUTLINE OF THE HISTORY OF "CHRISTIAN" ANTI-SEMITISM

of Kaiser Wilhelm II and sold almost one million copies in the German language. It proclaimed the German people as the "Aryan" master race and urged a crusade against all Jews, who were portrayed as vicious culture destroyers. One quote from this book says that "the Jewish race is altogether bastardized, and its existence is a crime against the holy laws of life…" This book had a major influence on Nazi racial ideology and Anti-Semitism.

These authors reflected a cultural and nationalist agenda based on ethnicity. This is known as ethno-nationalism which has been used often with lethal results and can be seen in many, if not most, countries throughout history. In combination with this was the belief in Social Darwinism, which taught that human evolution resulted from conflicts in which the most superior groups must either suppress or eradicate the lesser ones and thus purify the gene pool. This was used to justify the *final solution*. The ideal Nazi was blond and blue-eyed. Ironically none of the top Nazi leadership was either blond or had blue eyes.

In areas influenced by the Catholic and the Russian Orthodox Church, Jews continued to suffer religious, social, economic and political restrictions, discriminatory taxation, forced conversion, expulsion, ghettoization, plunder and slaughter.

The League of Anti-Semites, the Social Reich Party and the Agrarian League were Anti-Semitic political parties. They focused on Anti-Semitism as their main motive for achieving their political goals and the solution for all national ills.

Theodor Fritsch's Anti-Semitic writings did much to influence popular German opinion against Jews in the late 19th and early 20th centuries. In his book, *The Anti-Semitic Catechism*, there is a list of charges against Jews. These included:

- Usurious dealings with peasants and artisans
- Unfair business practices that were ruining honest business-men
- Destroying handicraft industries and creating wage slaves

- Forcing wages and prices down to the point that revolution was a constant threat
- Monopolizing the press and deceiving people by attacking legitimate authority
- Degrading national culture with sensationalism and obsceneity
- Committing fraud during the financial crash
- Contaminating legislatures
- Commercializing all values and running white slave trade
- Luring and bribing prominent persons
- Dominating all states through financial operations

Russia

Long-standing repressive policies and attitudes towards the Jews in Russia were intensified after the assassination of Tsar Alexander II in 1881. This event was blamed on the Jews and sparked widespread Anti-Jewish pogroms in the Russian Empire, which lasted for three years. It also resulted in the May Laws of 1882, which severely restricted the civil rights of Jews. The goal of these laws was that one third of the Jews would die out, one third would leave the country and one third would be assimilated. The result of these laws was horrific pogroms that led to mass emigration of Jews to Western Europe and America. From 1881 to 1914, (when the First World War began), an estimated 2.5 million Jews left Eastern Europe – one of the largest mass migrations in recorded history.

Russian Pogrom

PART 2 – AN OUTLINE OF THE HISTORY OF "CHRISTIAN" ANTI-SEMITISM

France

The defeat of France in the Franco-Prussian War (1870–1871) was partially attributed to the Jews. They were accused of weakening the national spirit through association with republicanism, capitalism and Anti-clericalism, particularly by authoritarian, right wing, clerical and royalist groups. These accusations were spread in Anti-Semitic journals such as La Libre Parole and La Croix, a Catholic publication. Financial scandals such as the collapse of the Union Generale Bank and the collapse of the French Panama Canal operation were also blamed on the Jews.

The Dreyfus Affair

Captain Alfred Dreyfus, a French Jewish army captain, was charged with selling military secrets to the Germans. He was court-martialed, found guilty and branded a traitor to France. Although he continued to proclaim his innocence, Captain Dreyfus was sentenced to life imprisonment on Devil's Island.

In 1896-1897, his case increasingly became the focus for political and ethnic struggles in French society. When the Chief of the Army Intelligence uncovered evidence of Dreyfus' innocence, he was removed from his position and transferred out of France. In 1898, the famous novelist Èmile Zola published *J'accuse!*, an open letter to the president of the French republic. The letter proclaimed Dreyfus' innocence and accused the military officers of deliberately framing Dreyfus. Zola was found guilty of libel for writing the article! After many legal battles Dreyfus was eventually granted a presidential pardon.

This case was significant because it brought to light the fact that Anti-Semitism ran throughout every level of European culture. In this case, it had been cunningly utilized as the catalyst for a counter-revolution to destroy the French Republic and restore the monarchy that had been abolished in 1871.

The Muslim World

In the 19th century, the position of Jews worsened in Muslim countries. Most scholars conclude that Arab Anti-Semitism in the modern world arose in the nineteenth century in conjunction with emerging and conflicting Jewish and Arab nationalism. There was a massacre of Jews in Baghdad in 1828. In 1839, in the Iranian city of Meshed, a mob burned the synagogue and destroyed the Torah scrolls. It was only by forced conversion that a massacre was averted.

In another Iranian city, Barfurush, there was a massacre of Jews in 1867. In 1840 the Jews of Damascus were falsely accused of having ritually murdered a Christian monk and his Muslim servant and of having used their blood to bake Passover unleavened bread. In 1864, around 500 Jews were killed in Marrakech and Fez in Morocco.

In 1869, 18 Jews were killed in Tunis. An Arab mob looted Jewish homes and stores and burned synagogues on Jerba Island. Jews in Morocco were attacked and killed in the streets in broad daylight. In 1891, the leading Muslims in Jerusalem asked the Ottoman authorities in Constantinople to prohibit the entry of Jews arriving from Russia.

20th Century Anti-Semitism

The 20th Century, perhaps more than any other, is the century of Anti-Semitism. It was a century of change. The old orders of life in Europe were removed and replaced. Two world wars, the demise of royalty, international economic upheaval, the emergence of modern science, psychology and Communism changed the entire European world on almost every level.

Russia

In 1903, a publication entitled *Protocols of the Learned Elders of Zion* appeared. This forgery was created by the Czarist secret police to justify their persecution of the Jews. This best seller accused the Jewish people of fostering an *international conspiracy* to control the world. As such, it became the justification for horrendous persecution.

This liberalist document was part of the foundation for Nazism. Despite its obvious absurdity it was widely believed, and tragically still is, particularly in the Islamic world.

During the years that the atheistic Communists controlled Russia and their satellite European countries, Jews suffered various kinds of state-sponsored Anti-Semitic oppression and persecution. They were prevented from practicing their religion and from emigrating. The number and kinds of incidents are too numerous for this book. You can easily find them online.

Nazi Germany

Because the Nazi persecution of the Jews is the defining and most scarring event of the modern Jewish world, I will present it in specific detail in its own section.

Latin America

The roots of Anti-Semitism in Latin America go back to the persecution of the Jews by the Spanish Catholics and to the secular racism of post enlightenment Europe. Countries like Brazil and Argentina opened their doors to many former Nazis. Mengele died in Brazil and Eichmann was captured in Argentina. The present Israeli-Palestinian conflict, as it does around the world, stirs up those roots and causes occasional outbreaks of Anti-Semitic incidents.

America

Between 1881 and 1920, approximately two million Jews fleeing persecution in Eastern Europe immigrated to America. Jews, like many other immigrants, faced discrimination in the United States in employment, education and social advancement. Groups like the Immigration Restriction League criticized these new arrivals as culturally, intellectually, morally and biologically inferior. Jews were blamed for the evils of capitalism and industrialism, and accused of controlling the economy via their international banking connections.

In 1915 Leo Frank, manager of the National Pencil Company in Atlanta, Georgia, was accused of murdering a 14-year-old girl. He pleaded innocent but was convicted and sentenced to hang. During his trial, vicious Anti-Semitic tirades were hurled against him and the Jewish community. On August 16th, 25 men entered the State Prison Farm and abducted and then lynched Leo Frank. No attempt was made to find the killers. Many Jews then left Atlanta. This incident revealed the Anti-Semitism that was operating in America at that time. Frank's lynching led to the founding of the Jewish Anti-Defamation League, as well as to renewed support for the racial hate group, the Ku Klux Klan.

Anti-Semitism in the United States reached its peak during the 1920s and 1930s. Henry Ford, Charles Lindberg and radio preacher Father Coughlin were some of the leading voices who expressed Anti-Semitic views. There were also those who created a German-American coalition that supported Hitler and the Nazis. In 1939, the American government tragically refused to allow the S.S. St. Louis, a ship with over 900 Jewish refugees from Germany, to disembark. Forced to return to Europe, many died in the Holocaust. During the Second World War, Anti-Semitism in the State Department and among some prominent elected national leaders created official resistance to helping Jews escape Nazi persecution. How many could have been saved if they would have allowed Jewish immigration?

Anti-Semitic groups continue in various forms of expression in

America.

21st Century Anti-Semitism

Anti-Semitism continues in the 21st century. Jewish and non-Jewish publications, blogs and websites regularly report accounts of Anti-Semitic vitriol. Physical attacks on Jews and Jewish institutions are regularly reported. Most are perpetrated by radical Muslim youths. A quick search of the internet will reveal how many Anti-Semitic websites exist. Views of the comment sections of various reports and blogs will show how much Anti-Semitic venom there exists in people's hearts. Europe's burgeoning Muslim population (enhanced by the present massive wave of illegal immigrants) will make it difficult for Jews to continue to live there. Watch for major Jewish emigration to Israel in fulfillment of Biblical prophecy (Psalm 107:3; Isaiah 54:7; Jeremiah 29:14; Ezekiel 36:24 - just to mention a few verses).

The state of Israel is the main target of present day Anti-Semitism. While there remains a legitimate place for disagreement with her governmental policies, Anti-Semitic attacks blame Israel for all the woes of the Middle East. These Anti-Semites conveniently ignore how much Muslim-to-Muslim hatred and violence there is. They seek to undermine Israel's legitimacy and ignore or reject the Jewish people's 3,000-year-long historical and Biblical right to their ancient homeland. Israel is denigrated as a *Western imperialistic colonial usurper of Arab lands.*

Radical Muslim hatred for Israel and the Jewish people continues unabated. Ranging from almost daily outlandish verbal attacks by Muslim clerics (see www.memritv.org), to the production of Anti-Semitic TV programs, to the constant vilifying of Jews as *pigs and sons of monkeys*, in Muslim newspapers and magazines and even in children's textbooks, the demonic spirits of Anti-Semitism are busy at work.

We must take seriously the Iranian threat to destroy the nation of Israel. Iran will continue to work toward the creation of nuclear weapons and the missiles capable of delivering them, regardless of any deals they make with the West.

This demonically inspired Anti-Semitism seeks not only the destruction of the state of Israel, but as it always has, the annihilation of the Jewish people (Psalm 83:4; Esther 3:6). However, their end will be like that promised to Amalek, the Biblical representative of all Anti-Semitically inspired people: total destruction (Numbers 24:20; see also Exodus 17:8-16).

Of course, what is different today from any other historical period is that the Jewish people are neither stateless nor politically, economically or socially powerless. Israel continues to be a leader in technology and Jews keep winning Nobel prizes! Israel certainly has the strongest, most sophisticated military in the Middle East.

But remember, dear reader, this battle against Anti-Semitism is not *"against flesh and blood"* but is a *"battle against principalities, powers, and spiritual wickedness in high places"* (Ephesians 6:12), that seek to prevent the prophetic purposes of God from being fulfilled, and if they could, prevent the return of Yeshua (Jesus).

The Islamic World

Any study of the history of Islam and the Jews will reveal that there have been times when the Jews prospered under Islamic rule, as well as times of attacks upon the Jewish people. For the purposes of brevity in this book, I again refer you to online studies, as there are many websites available for you on this subject. As you read you must understand that fanatical Islamic fundamentalism poses not only a grave danger to the Jews and the Nation of Israel, but to all freedom-loving people around the world. Remember the stated goal of these radical fundamentalist Muslims is the conversion of the world to their version of Islam by any means necessary.

PART 2 – AN OUTLINE OF THE HISTORY OF "CHRISTIAN" ANTI-SEMITISM

Categories of Anti-Semitic Persecution

In these sections are examples of where and when Anti-Semitic incidents took place, as well as the many other years Jews suffered these types of persecution. This will give you some idea of just how many *scarring* experiences the Jewish people have endured.

1) Anti-Semitism Enacted into Law or State Policy

Date	Place	Description
306	Spain	The Church Synod of Elvira banned all community contacts between Christians and Jews.
315	Italy	The Roman Emperor Constantine published the Edict of Milan which extended religious tolerance to Christians. Jews lost many rights with this edict. They were no longer permitted to live in Jerusalem or to proselytize.
325	Turkey	The Council of Nicaea with its theological Anti-Judaism laid the groundwork for Anti-Semitic legislation of later church councils. For example, here it was decided to celebrate the resurrecttion of Jesus on the pagan based *Easter* rather than the Biblical date of Passover. This counsel declared that: **"It is unbecoming beyond measure that on this holiest of festivals we should follow the customs of the Jews. Henceforth let us have nothing in common with this odious people...We ought not, therefore, to have anything in common with the Jews...our worship follows a...more convenient**

Date	Place	Description
		course...we desire dearest brethren, to separate ourselves from the detestable company of the Jews...How, then, could we follow these Jews, who are almost certainly blinded."
		The Council of Antioch (341) prohibited Christians from celebrating Passover with the Jews.
		The Council of Laodicea (363) forbade Christians from observing the Jewish Sabbath. Christians were also forbidden from receiving gifts from Jews or Matzo from Passover celebrations.
516	France	In Burgundy, King Sigismund converted to Christianity and introduced oppression of Jews as state policy.
528	Rome	Emperor Justinian developed what came to be known as the Justinian Code. This Code made Church law and doctrine state policy. The Code limited the civil and religious liberties of Jews, including assembling in public; forbade them to have Christian slaves, to testify against Christians in court or to celebrate Passover before Easter. It prohibited Jews from building synagogues, reading the Bible in Hebrew and prohibited prayers seen as Anti-Trinitarian.
845	France	Church leaders called the Council of Meaux, which re-established old canonical laws and Anti-Jewish restrictions, hoping that Emperor Charles the Bald would make them state policy. Jews

PART 2 – AN OUTLINE OF THE HISTORY OF "CHRISTIAN" ANTI-SEMITISM

Date	**Place**	**Description**
		were not to hold public office or be seen in public during Easter week. Charles refused then dissolved the Council.
1241	Spain	King Fernando III instituted the Visigothic Code of 634, *Liber Iudiciorum*, "legal code" (translated into Spanish as "Fuero Juzgo"). This law forbade Jews, under severe penalty, from practicing their religion. This led to mass forced conversions and further decrees of death for practicing Judaism secretly.
1265	Spain	King Alfonso X established the legal code, *Las Siete Partidas* (the "Seven-Part Code"). It stated, "The reason that the church, emperors, kings and princes allow the Jews to dwell among them and with Christians is this: that they might always live in captivity, and thus be a reminder to all that they are descended from those who crucified Our Lord Jesus Christ."
1804	Russia	Czar Alexander I passed a series of laws whose effects were disastrous for the Jews. Article 34 ordered that within 3 to 4 years, Jews would be forbidden to reside in the villages. Over 60,000 families (about half a million people) were affected. The laws were implemented in mid-winter, but no provisions were made for helping the evicted population. This resulted in the deaths of many by starvation or exposure.
1862	America	During the Civil War, Major General

Date	Place	Description
		Ulysses S. Grant issued orders removing Jews from the Treasury Department.
1878	Germany/ Romania	Adolph Stoecker founded the Christian Socialist Workers Party. His appeals included social reforms, state socialism and Anti-Semitism. Despite provisions of the Congress of Berlin which granted Jews equal rights, the Romanian government passed discriminatory laws. Two hundred such laws passed, barring Jews from various trades and professions and from living in the villages. When required to move to urban ghettos, the horror of possible starvation caused 125,000 to emigrate to the U.S.
1882	Russia	Temporary Rules of 1882 (May Laws) provided: 1. No new Jewish settlements were permitted outside the villages of the Pale (area of settlement for Jews). 2. No Jews were to buy, lease or manage real estate or farms outside the cities of the Pale. 3. No Jew was to transact business on Sunday or on any other Christian holiday. These *temporary rules* were in effect for 35 years.
1889	Russia	Jews were barred from almost every profession. Hundreds of Jews who had completed their legal education or who were assistants to attorneys were prevented from practicing law.

PART 2 – AN OUTLINE OF THE HISTORY OF "CHRISTIAN" ANTI-SEMITISM

Date	**Place**	**Description**
1915	Russia	The Commander-in-Chief of Russia's military ordered 600,000 Jews living in the Pale to be forcibly relocated to the interior of Russia. Their homes and businesses were looted and burned. Approximately 100,000 Jews died from exposure or starvation during the relocation.
1921	America	Between 1881 and 1914, approximately 1,450,000 Jews immigrated to America. President Harding called a special session of Congress to rewrite the immigration laws in an effort to stem immigration to the U.S.

2) Official Charges Lodged Against Jews

Charges were lodged in years: 300, 415, 1144, 1168, 1171, 1180, 1181, 1183, 1192, 1244, 1247, 1255, 1276, 1283, 1285, 1294, 1422, 1431, 1453, 1475, 1480, 1485, 1491, 1510, 1540, 1598, 1636, 1639, 1657, 1660, 1670, 1698, 1710, 1736, 1747, 1748, 1759, 1840, 1850, 1855, 1878, 1882, 1889, 1891, 1899, 1900, 1911, 1926, 1927 and 1928.

a) Deicide

One of the most persistent accusations used to persecute the Jewish people was that all Jews everywhere throughout history were collectively guilty of the crime of *Deicide* – Killing God. In blaming Jews as *Christ-Killers* all manner of Anti-Semitic acts were perpetrated. The earliest recorded instance of this accusation occurred in a sermon of 167 attributed to Melito of Sardis entitled *Peri Pascha, On the Passover*. The Latin word *deicida* (slayer of god), from which the word *deicide* is derived, was first used in the 4th century by Peter Chrysologus. You will find this accusation repeated endlessly throughout church history. Thankfully most major Christian denominations have repudiated this horrific lie, although you can still hear it mentioned and believed in some Christian churches.

It was the Romans who tortured and crucified Jesus. The New Testament clearly shows us that while it is true that some Jewish leaders and their immediate followers were complicit in the betrayal and death of Jesus, it was certainly not the entire Jewish nation. This is not to mitigate their responsibility. The preaching of the apostles to the Jewish people makes this very clear. The apostle Peter declared that the leaders of the nation, and those who conspired with them, though they "*acted in ignorance*" they did in fact "*reject the Holy and Righteous One,*" "*nailing Him to a cross by the hands of godless men,*" and are culpable for "*killing the Author of Life*" who "*God then raised from the dead*" (Acts 2:23, 3:14-18).

It is extremely important to remember that the suffering of the Messiah as an atonement for humanities sins and His rejection by the Jewish leadership was all according to the preordained plan of God (Isaiah 53; Psalm 22;12-18; John 3:16; Acts 2:23; 1 Corinthians 15:3; Revelation 13:8). Jesus declared that "*no one could take His life*" as He voluntarily surrendered Himself to be the "*Lamb of God who takes away the sins of the world*" (John 1:29, 10:14-18; Luke 24:27; Acts 3:18, 26:22; 1 Peter 1:20). He also asked God to forgive His betrayers and executioners because they did it not knowing what they were doing (Luke 23:34). Additionally, the rejection of Jesus by the Jewish people is part of God's plan to bring the Gospel to the Nations (Romans 11:11-12).

The devil, as he always tries to do, perverted God's truth and used it as a weapon for his evil purposes. Nowhere in the New Testament is it even remotely hinted at that all Jews everywhere for all time are guilty of the crime of deicide. It is only the enemies of God's purposes for the Jewish people who used the death of Jesus as an excuse for perpetrating their satanically inspired evil persecutions and murders.

There is no place in the New Testament where the Church, or individual Christians, are called to be instruments of judgment and punishment. Everything done in the Name of Jesus to harm the Jewish people was in direct contradiction to the clear teaching of the New Testament. Christians are called to be a people of *"love and good works"* (1 Corinthians 13; Matthew 5:16; Ephesians 2:10; 1Timothy 6:17) who are *"ambassadors of reconciliation"* that reflect and represent God's desire for all people to enter into His Kingdom (2 Corinthians 5:17-21).

Everything done in opposition to these fundamental truths is built upon satanically inspired deception and lies.

b) **Ritual Murder**

Another of Satan's accusations against the Jewish people was that the Jews sought revenge upon the Christians by re-enacting the crucifixion of Jesus through the ritual murder of a Christian child. This horrific lie told that the Jews murdered a child and drained the blood to use in the baking of Matzos (unleavened bread) for the festival of Passover. They were also accused of drinking it in the course of the Passover Seder.

Superstitious and ignorant people believed this horrific lie, and Church leaders used it to inflame them to acts of violence against the Jews as a way of "honoring" the name of Jesus. This is another accusation that the devil perversely used as a way to persecute the Jews and to make Jesus an anathema to the Jewish people.

Various punishments for this imaginary "crime" included exorbitant taxes or ransom payments, different forms of excruciating torture, imprisonment, hanging and burning alive. From the year 300 to the year 1928 there were at least 50 different incidents of this charge being made.

c) Well Poisoning

The Jewish people were accused of poisoning wells. The alleged poisons were supposedly made from spiders, frogs and lizards, from the hearts of murdered Christians or from stolen Communion wafers. Based on these demonic accusations, Jews were tortured, burned at the stake, expelled or forcibly baptized. In one incident a thousand Jews in cities near the border of Poland and Germany were slaughtered by so called "Christian" mobs, despite the royal protection King Casimir attempted to afford them.

Date	Place	Description
1348	France	In Toulon, a Jewish congregation, including men, women and children together with their holy writings, were burned alive.
1348	Spain	In Catalonia, Aragon and Barcelona, Jews were murdered by mobs which plundered Jewish homes.
1348	Switzerland	Duke Amadeus of Savoy commanded the arrest of several Jews suspected of poisoning wells in two small towns. Under torture they confessed. As a consequence, all Jews in the region of Lake Geneva and Savoy were burned at the stake.
1348	Germany	More than 350 Jewish communities were destroyed as a result of being accused of poisoning wells and causing the Black Death. Tens of thousands of men, women and children were tortured and killed.

PART 2 – AN OUTLINE OF THE HISTORY OF "CHRISTIAN" ANTI-SEMITISM

Date	Place	Description
1357	Germany	In Franconia, Jews were blamed for causing the black plague by poisoning wells.
1571	Germany	A Jewish minister of finance in Brandenburg was charged with embezzlement. Under torture, he confessed to all manner of crimes including sorcery and well poisoning. The confession was recanted at his trial, but under further torture he again confessed. He was executed and the Jewish community there was attacked by roving mobs. Their property was confiscated and they were expelled.

d) Host Desecration

Charges were lodged in years: 1298, 1308, 1354, 1367, 1377, 1399, 1408, 1422, 1453, 1475, 1491, 1510, 1556 and 1637.

Building upon the accusation that the Jews were "Christ Killers" was the persistent false charge of "Host Desecration." This demonic allegation was based upon the unscriptural Catholic doctrine known as "Transubstantiation." This doctrine, and its name, was formally adopted at the Fourth Lateran Council in 1215. The Catholic Church teaches that during the Mass, the priest "miraculously transforms" the elements of Communion (the wafer and wine) into the literal body and blood of Jesus, although the external appearance and substance of the elements remains the same. The wafer now becomes the "Host" – the actually body of Jesus.

The Jewish people were not only being blamed for the crucifixion of Jesus, this demonic lie, yet another example of a 'doctrine of demons,' proclaimed that the Jews nurtured in their hearts such an undying hatred for Jesus that it became a diabolical obsession which motivated them to continually seek to reenact the crucifixion symbolically by secretly stealing the Host from the Church altar, and then gleefully and cruelly piercing, burning, and defiling the "holy wafer," with sharp knives, needles, and other pointed objects. And where else could it take place but in the holy sanctuary of the synagogue, right before the Ark containing the Torah Scrolls.

Those Church leaders who propagated this demonic accusation told their people that Host Desecration was a "sacred Jewish rite." Whipping crowds into a fury, they proclaimed "This is what the Jews are doing to our lovely Lord Jesus. They are crucifying Him again." The result was always the same. Inflamed "Christian" mobs ransacked Jewish communities, maiming and killing men, women and children, who were completely innocent.

"Host" Desecration

PART 2 – AN OUTLINE OF THE HISTORY OF "CHRISTIAN" ANTI-SEMITISM

Woodcuts, like the one above from the Middle Ages, depict the act of Host Desecration. Jews, identified by typical Jewish dress, are seen stabbing the Host and watching it bleed. Church authorities used this accusation to once again, incite the ignorant superstitious masses into violent mobs.

Date	**Place**	**Description**
1298	Germany	The accusation of Host Desecration with the *miraculous bleeding* of the Host in the town of Bavaria launched one of the most severe persecutions in this area.
1308	France	The Bishop of Strasbourg demanded that the Jews charged with desecrating a Host be burned alive.
1377	Spain	In Huesca, Jews charged with desecrating a Host were tortured and burned at the stake.
1399	Poland	In Posen, Jews were charged with bribing a Christian woman to steal Hosts from a local church. Allegedly, the Hosts were stabbed, bled and thrown into a pit. The Archbishop learned of the "blasphemy" and ordered that the Rabbi, 13 elders and the woman be tied to pillars and roasted alive over a slow fire.
1510	Germany	Ritual murder and Host Desecration accusations were made in Brandenburg. Thirty Jews were tortured and burned alive.

3) Proselytizing Prohibited

Laws enacted in: 325, 538, 545, 612 and 1539.

One way that Church authorities exercised control over their people was by keeping them illiterate. If they were not completely illiterate, they were banned from studying the Scriptures. Generally speaking, all Jews were literate and could read and understand the Hebrew Scriptures. Because of this knowledge, Jews were a threat to those Church authorities and were therefore forbidden to talk to Christians about their faith. If a Jew tried to convert a Christian to Judaism, he was liable to the death penalty and the confiscation of his property.

The Third and Fourth Councils of Orléans (France, in 538) commanded Christians not to take part in Jewish holidays and forbade Jews to proselytize or to appear in public during the Easter period. Christians who participated in the Biblical Feasts of the Lord with Jews faced punishment. Satan has been determined since the beginning of the Church to keep Christians and Jews in a mutually hostile and adversarial relationship.

Date	**Place**	**Description**
614	Spain	Full-scale persecution of Jews in Spain was begun by a decree issued by King Sisebut. Jews who refused baptism were severely and cruelly punished. Ninety-thousand were forcibly baptized. He would later require all Jews to convert or leave the country.
1539	Poland	In Krakow, many rumors circulated that Christians were converting to Judaism and moving to the greater safety of Lithuania. The Polish king sent investigators to Lithuania and Jewish homes were raided and travelers were arrested.

4) Confiscation of Property

These incidents took place in the years: 357, 582, 681, 693, 694, 897, 1239, 1240, 1254, 1272, 1278, 1293, 1306, 1311, 1313, 1360,

PART 2 – AN OUTLINE OF THE HISTORY OF "CHRISTIAN" ANTI-SEMITISM

1366, 1377, 1390, 1391, 1422, 1453, 1495, 1509, 1554, 1555, 1571, 1655, 1670 and 1775.

Date	Place	Description
357	Rome	Emperor Constantine passed a law that confiscated all property of any Christian who converted to Judaism.
693-694	Spain	The Sixteenth and Seventeenth Councils of Toledo required the Jews to turn over to the royal treasury all property ever acquired from Christian owners.
1239	England	A Jew was accused of murder in London and a bloody riot started. A number of Jews were imprisoned and several were put to death. One third of the entire community's property was confiscated as punishment - because *one* Jew was just accused of a murder.
1239	Rome	Pope Gregory IX ordered all copies of the Talmud[46] confiscated in France, England, Castile, Aragon and Portugal.
1240-1242	France/ England	After a public "disputation" between a Jewish "convert," Nicolas Donin, and leading Rabbis (the Rabbis had no chance of winning), King Louis IX (St. Louis) of France carried out a papal order for confiscation of the Talmud. All Jewish books in England were seized, and the Talmud was burned in accordance with this papal decree.

---

[46] A collection of 63 volumes containing the Jewish civil and canonical law in the form of interpretation and expansion of the teachings of the Old Testament. The word Talmud means "instruction."

Date	Place	Description
1254	France	Jews were expelled from France by King Louis IX. All Jewish property, synagogues and cemeteries were confiscated.
1495	Lithuania	Jews were expelled and their property confiscated and distributed among local Christians. However, the Jews were permitted to return in 1501 and some property was returned.
1509	Germany	John Pffefferkorn was a Jewish convert to Christianity. But he was never truly converted in his heart, because instead of loving the Jewish people and proclaiming the Good News of Salvation to them, he launched attacks on Jewish communities. In one incident he received permission from Emperor Maximilian to examine all Jewish books for the purpose of destroying all that the Church considered to be blasphemous or hostile to Christianity. All religious books found in synagogues or in house-to-house searches of the Jewish quarter in Frankfurt were confiscated. More than 1,500 books were seized.
1670	Austria	Emperor Leopold banished all Jews from Vienna. Violation of the order was punishable by death. All Jewish property was sold and later that year all Jews were expelled from the rest of Austria.

PART 2 – AN OUTLINE OF THE HISTORY OF "CHRISTIAN" ANTI-SEMITISM

5) **Destruction of Property**

These incidents took place in the years: 351, 506, 1009, 1242, 1389, 1553, 1559, 1592, 1615, 1648, 1757, 1764, 1775, 1793, 1850, 1866, 1881, 1915, 1923, 1929 and 1932.

Date	Place	Description
506	Antioch	The synagogue at Daphne (near Antioch) was destroyed. Holy items were desecrated and the congregation was slaughtered by a "Christian" mob celebrating the outcome of the chariot races.
1242	France	In Paris, 24 cartloads of the Talmud were burned on numerous occasions in various places.
1389	Bohemia	In Prague, following an accusation of Host Desecration, over 900 Jewish people were killed and all of their possessions confiscated. The Synagogue, Torah Scrolls and sacred books were burned.
1553	Rome	Pope Julius III approved and signed a decree presented by the Inquisitor General ordering the seizure of the Talmud. On September 9 (the Jewish New Year) all copies of the Talmud and compilations from it in Rome were burned. The same occurred in many other cities. Other Hebrew books, including the Bible, were also burned.
1615	Germany	The Jewish community was expelled from Worms. The synagogue and cemetery were destroyed.

Date	Place	Description
1757	Russia	The Bishop of Kamenetz ordered all copies of the Talmud burned. As a result, nearly 1,000 copies of the Talmud were destroyed.
1866	Romania	A mob gathered in Bucharest to prevent granting of equal citizenship to Jews. Synagogues and sacred writings were desecrated and destroyed.
1929	Poland	Jewish high school girls were accused of mocking a Catholic procession. As a result, groups of young Catholics and university students attacked the Jewish quarter in Lemburg. Ten synagogues, numerous Jewish homes and shops in the quarter were vandalized.
1923-1932	Germany	One hundred and twenty-eight Jewish cemeteries and fifty synagogues were vandalized.

6) Discrimination and Unjust Taxation

These incidents took place in the years: 70, 79, 81, 506, 681, 981, 996, 1130, 1144, 1194, 1232, 1244, 1275, 1281, 1313, 1348, 1392, 1434, 1442, 1451, 1499, 1515, 1555, 1562, 1641, 1670, 1725, 1727, 1772, 1780, 1790, 1791, 1794, 1800, 1808, 1809, 1811, 1819, 1820, 1823, 1827, 1877, 1881, 1894, 1895, 1902, 1914, 1920, 1922, 1927, 1931, 1934, 1935, 1936, 1937 and 1938.

Scores of instances of legalized discrimination and unjust taxation have taken place. Christians were excommunicated and discriminated against as a punishment for associating with Jewish people in any way. In England, in 1275, you could be excommunicated from the Church just for attending a Jewish wedding!

PART 2 – AN OUTLINE OF THE HISTORY OF "CHRISTIAN" ANTI-SEMITISM

Date	**Place**	**Description**
70	Judea	The Roman Emperor Vespasian initiated collection of the temple tax, continuing the practice of using the Jew as a special taxpayer and source of revenue.
79-81	Judea	The temple tax now served as a fee for a license to practice Judaism.
1232	England	Exorbitant taxes were levied against the Jews of England.
1360	Spain	Don Henry de Trastamara cancelled all debts owed by Christians to Jews, and levied a fine of 50,000 doubloons on the Jewish community in Castile. The Jews were forced to sell their property, belongings and religious artifacts to pay this debt. Many Jews were sold into slavery.
1434	Switzerland	The Council of Basle decreed that Jews should live in *separate sections of the city*.
1442	Spain	In Castile, Pope Eugenius IV forbade Christians to eat, drink, bathe, live with Jews or to use medicine of any kind prescribed by Jews. Jews were ineligible for any office or honor. No new synagogues were to be built, and in repairing existing synagogues, ornamentation was prohibited. Jews were required to remain indoors during Easter. Testimony of Jews against Christians was declared in-

Date	Place	Description
		valid.[47] Jews were distinguished from Christians by *special dress* and special quarters.
1451	Italy & Spain	Pope Nicholas V issued a bull[48] excluding Italian and Spanish Jews from Christian society and from all honorable professions.
1499	Germany	Nuremberg expelled the city's Jewish community. Similar expulsions took place throughout the country. The only Jewish communities remaining in Germany were in Ratisbon, Frankfurt on Main and Worms. These were under constant threat of expulsion and daily harassment. Millers and bakers refused to sell to Jews. Clergy threatened tradesmen with excommunication should they trade with the Jews.[49] Jews could shop in the market only on certain days and only during specified hours.
1514-1515	France	In Strasbourg, royal judgements banished Jews. These laws remained in effect until the end of the 18th century.
1520	Italy	In Venice, the agreement allowing Jews to remain was renewed, but tax of

---

[47] In other words, you could commit a crime against a Jew, and any testimony that Jews gave against you would be invalid. Those who committed crimes against Jews were not punished.

[48] A bull is an order issued by the Pope. To Catholics, this is considered a divine command.

[49] In many places, Christians were forbidden to be involved in any commerce with Jews.

PART 2 – AN OUTLINE OF THE HISTORY OF "CHRISTIAN" ANTI-SEMITISM

Date	Place	Description
		10,000 ducats per year was levied.
1604	Netherlands	In Amsterdam, Jewish funeral processions had to pay a tax to each church they passed on the way to the cemetery.
1612	Germany	In Hamburg, the state granted Portuguese Jews free residence in the city for an annual *protection fee* of 1,000 marks. They were not allowed to have a synagogue or to conduct religious services or circumcision privately. They were, however, allowed to bury their dead in their own cemetery.
1641	Germany	Civil and economic restrictions were applied to the Jewish community in Worms.
1664	Poland	Students of the Cathedral school and the Jesuit Academy of Lemberg organized an attack on the Jewish quarter. About 100 Jews were killed and much of the quarter was destroyed and the synagogues were desecrated. For protection against such attacks, the Jewish communities paid an annual tax to the local Catholic schools.
1790	France	The French National Assembly denied the Jews of France the right to vote.
1791	Russia	Catherine the Great decreed that Jews could be citizens in White Russia only. They could not register as merchants in the towns and seaports of the rest of the Empire. Within the Pale (area of settlement for Jews), taxes on Jews were

Date	Place	Description
		double those for Christians.
1794	Russia	Jews are further restricted and additionally taxed. They cannot move from cities without paying a double tax or face expulsion. They are forbidden from serving in the military, but have to pay a special tax for this "privilege."
1800	America	Provisions in most state constitutions require office holders to believe in the divinity of Jesus. This effectively barred Jews from holding state and local political offices.
1823	Rome	Pope Leo XII re-established the ghetto system. Napoleon had previously opened the ghettos during his occupation of Italy.
1823	Russia	In April, the Czar forbade the Jews in some provinces to hold land leases or to run public houses or inns. All contracts to the contrary were voided. He ordered all Jews to be resettled in the towns and cities by January 1, 1825.
1902	New York	During a funeral procession for Rabbi Jacob Joseph in New York City, workers in a printing press factory threw hot metal and refuse down onto the marchers. A riot occurred and many Jews were injured by the police.
1922	Massachusetts	The President of Harvard University called for a quota on Jewish admissions to relieve university overcrowding. The Trustees defeated the quota plan, but an

PART 2 – AN OUTLINE OF THE HISTORY OF "CHRISTIAN" ANTI-SEMITISM

Date	Place	Description
		unofficial Jewish quota was adopted and spread to many colleges, universities and professional schools.
1934	Canada	Anti-Jewish groups were formed throughout Canada urging boycotts of Jewish labor and stores.
1935	Lithuania	Jews were banned from the University of Kaunas medical school.
1939	Romania	By the end of 1939, Romania had removed Jews from economic participation in their society. Jewish factory workers had been discharged, and Jewish doctors and lawyers were prohibited from practicing.
1940	Occupied Europe	Separate ghettos were created one by one in the territories conquered by the Nazis.

7) Segregation

These incidents took place in the years: 306, 320, 429, 465, 506, 517, 535, 545, 581, 589, 615, 692, 740, 945, 1078, 1081, 1179, 1228, 1279, 1412, 1434, 1494, 1496, 1516, 1540, 1555, 1567, 1610, 1613, 1617, 1619, 1638, 1650, 1667, 1676, 1679, 1693, 1759, 1794, 1815, 1821, 1823, 1841, 1843, 1848, 1867 and 1937.

Date	Place	Description
429	Italy	Emperor Honorius barred Jews from public and military office in Rome.
506	Italy	In Rome, Jews were forbidden to hold public office, intermarry with Christians, build new synagogues, own Christian slaves or prosecute apostates.

Date	Place	Description
615	France	King Clotaire II upheld the Council of Paris which forbade Jews to hold magisterial power or to enter military service.
1078	Rome	Pope Gregory VII barred Jews from any office in *Christendom* and from any supremacy over Christians.
1496	Italy	A regulation was passed preventing any Jew from staying in Venice for more than two weeks each year. After this limit was reached, a 12-month interval had to elapse before any further visits were permitted.
1516	Italy	**In Venice, all Jews were required to move to the Ghetto Nuovo, a small, dirty island. It became the world's first ghetto.** *Ghetto* is from the Italian *getto* meaning *casting* or Venetian *geto* meaning *foundry*.
1555	Italy	Pope Paul IV renewed the enforcement of canonical laws pertaining to Jews. Segregation in ghettos continued. Jews were barred from professions and forbidden to own real estate. Those who owned real estate were compelled to sell it within 6 months. Christians were not to be employed by Jews under threat of heavy penalties. Jewish physicians were forbidden to treat Christians.
1610	Italy	In Mantua, Jews were required to live in a walled ghetto. The gates of the ghetto

PART 2 – AN OUTLINE OF THE HISTORY OF "CHRISTIAN" ANTI-SEMITISM

Date	Place	Description
		were locked at sunset and unlocked at dawn.
1638	Italy	In Modena, the ghetto system was introduced.
1679	Italy	In Turin, the ghetto system of segregation was established.
1693	Italy	In Trieste the ghettos were established.
1759	Poland	In Lvov (Lemberg), Jews were forced to live in ghettos.
1815	Austria	The Emperor required Jews to live in ghettos.
1815	Rome	Pope Pius VII reinstituted the Inquisition. Jews in Papal States were driven back into ghettos and stripped of civil rights, liberties and positions granted by city republics.
1823	Rome	A new edict from Pope Leo XII forbade Jews from leaving their ghetto in Rome without a written permit.
1841	Russia	Czar Nicholas I ordered the establishment of special Jewish schools. Education in these schools was formulated to weaken the influence of the Talmud by teaching secular subjects and Jewish religion according to Russian Orthodox interpretation. Its purpose was to convert Jews to Russian Orthodoxy. Jews were prohibited from attending other schools.

Date	Place	Description
1843	Prussia	The government evicted thousands of families along the Austrian borders.
1867	Romania	Jews were forbidden to live in villages or to own inns or taverns.
1937	Poland	Jewish university students were required to sit in special segregated sections of classrooms.

8) Slander

These incidents took place in the years: 367, 376, 418, 638, 829, 887, 1040, 1399, 1542, 1553, 1654, 1773, 1794, 1800, 1844, 1845, 1855, 1868, 1871, 1872, 1874, 1875, 1879, 1880, 1881, 1886, 1887, 1888, 1889, 1890, 1892, 1893, 1899, 1905, 1908, 1911, 1917, 1918, 1920, 1921, 1924, 1928, 1931 and 1937.

Date	Place	Description
100-165	Rome	Justin Martyr, an early Christian apologist wrote that Jewish misfortunes were the result of divine punishment for "murdering the just one."
120-185	Sardis	Bishop Melito, this important leader in the church, accused the Jews of "murdering God."
367	France	St. Hilary of Poitiers characterized Jews as a perverse people forever accursed by God. **The Bible, however, says they are** *"beloved for the father's sake"* (Romans 11:28).
386	North Africa	**John Chrysostom, the Patriarch of Constantinople, known as the Bishop with the Golden tongue, taught that**

PART 2 – AN OUTLINE OF THE HISTORY OF "CHRISTIAN" ANTI-SEMITISM

Date	Place	Description
		the "Jews are the most worthless of men - they are lecherous, greedy, rapacious - they are perfidious murderers of Christians, they worship the devil, their religion is a sickness...The Jews are the odious assassins of Christ and for killing God there is no expiation, no indulgence, no pardon. Christians may never cease vengeance. The Jews must live in servitude forever. Since God hates the Jews, it is the duty of Christians to hate them, too. He who has no limits in his love of Christ must have no limits in his battle with those who hate Him. I hate the Jews. It is incumbent on all Christians to hate the Jews."

This is the opposite of what Jesus and both the Old and New Testaments teach. Jeremiah 31:3 says that God *"loves the Jewish people with an everlasting love."* Romans 11:28 teaches that the Jews are *"beloved for the sake of the fathers."* Here is a clear example of how people who claim to love Jesus can be deceived and influenced by "doctrines of demons" and "deceitful spirits" (1 Timothy 4:1). |
| 415 | North Africa | **St. Augustine** wrote, "The true image of the Hebrew is Judas Iscariot, who sells the Lord for silver. **The Jew can never understand the Scriptures and forever will bear the guilt for the death of Jesus.**" |

Date	Place	Description
418	Rome	**St. Jerome** (translator of the Vulgate Bible) wrote a *Tract against the Jews*, accusing them of being congenital liars who lure Christians to heresy and who should be punished until they confess. **He called the synagogue a "brothel, a den of vice, the Devil's refuge, Satan's fortress, a place to deprave the soul and an abyss of every conceivable disaster."** He also wrote, **"God hates the Jews and I hate the Jews."**

The writings of Saints Jerome, Chrysostom and Augustine are of special significance. They were not obscure leaders, but Fathers and Doctors of the Church, as important to the growth of what's called Christianity as were the Apostles. **Their Anti-Semitic writings had widespread and profound impact, and bestowed a sanctity and respectability on Anti-Semitism which bore horrific fruit.** |
638	Spain	Isadore, Bishop of Seville, and Julian, Bishop of Toledo, wrote polemical tracts against Judaism.
829	France	The Epistles of St. Agod, Archbishop of Lyons, "proved" that Jews were born slaves; that they were stealing Christian children and selling them to the Arabs; and that they are accursed by God and should be so regarded by all Christians.
1205	Italy	In Rome, Pope Innocent III declared that "the Jews, by their own guilt, are consigned to perpetual servitude be-

PART 2 – AN OUTLINE OF THE HISTORY OF "CHRISTIAN" ANTI-SEMITISM

Date	Place	Description
		cause they crucified the Lord...As slaves rejected by God, in whose death they wickedly conspired, they shall by the effect of this very action, recognize themselves as the slaves of those whom Christ's death set free..."
1271	Italy	Thomas Aquinas, one of the most influential thinkers of the medieval church, wrote in his *Letter on the Treatment of Jews*, "The Jews by reason of their crucifying the Lord are sentenced to perpetual servitude" and "Jews in all Christian provinces, and all the time, should be distinguished from other people by some clothing."
1390	England	Geoffrey Chaucer, the renowned English poet, wrote the anti-Semitic story *The Prioress's Tale* as part of his famous Canterbury Tales. This story accuses the Jews of the notorious "Blood Libel" and they are tortured and massacred. (As an interesting side note, two other famous English novels, *Ivanhoe* by Sir Walter Scott (1820), and *Daniel Deronda* by George Eliot (1876), speak against the mistreatment of the Jews and speak very positively of the Jewish people).
1517	Holland	The famous Dutch theologian, Erasmus, wrote, "If it is Christian to detest the Jews, on this count we are all good Christians, and to spare."
1542	Germany	**Luther** turned against the Jews. In his early career as the leader of the Reform-

Date	**Place**	**Description**
		ation, he had been very friendly toward the Jews and defended them against Catholic attempts to convert them. He wrote a very positive tract entitled *That Christ was born a Jew*, which expressed his hope that "if one deals in a kindly way with the Jews and instructs them carefully, many of them will become genuine Christians and turn again to the faith of their fathers, the prophets and patriarchs." However, as the Jewish people rejected his message, toward the end of his life his attitude changed completely and he published a book entitled *Concerning the Jews and Their Lies*.
		He urged the emperor and princes to expel Jews from the country without delay and to drive them back to their own land. If the nobility did not do so, it was the duty of the robber knights, the clergy and the people to subjugate or expel them.
1597	Geneva	The great theologian **John Calvin** showed himself somewhat more merciful toward the Jews than toward those he considered Christian heretics; however, he was also guilty of keeping the Jews out of Geneva and of slandering them. He wrote that "I have had much conversation with many Jews: I have never seen either a drop of piety or a grain of truth or ingenuousness – nay, I have never found common sense in any Jew." He is also quoted as calling Jews "profane dogs" who "under the pretext

PART 2 – AN OUTLINE OF THE HISTORY OF "CHRISTIAN" ANTI-SEMITISM

Date	**Place**	**Description**
		of prophecy, stupidly devour all the riches of the earth with their unrestrained cupidity." In his infamous small tract, *Ad Quaelstiones et Objecta Juaei Cuiusdam Responsio (A Re-sponse to Questions and Objections of a Certain Jew)*, he wrote: "The Jews' rotten and unbending stiffneckedness deserves that they be oppressed unendingly and without measure or end and that they die in their misery without the pity of anyone."
1654	New Amsterdam	Colonies of the New World were influenced by Anti-Semitic literature. On September 22, Peter Stuyvesant sent a letter to the West India Company, referring to the Jews as hateful enemies and as blasphemers of the name of Christ who should not be allowed to infect and trouble the new colony.
1794	America	Susanna Rowsom's *Slaves in Algiers: or A Struggle for Freedom,* the first play written and produced in America with a Jewish character, portrayed him as a scoundrel who changed his faith to Islam when it offered him monetary advantage. The play also portrayed the Jew as a forger and a crook, who cheated the Gentiles, because it was demanded by Moses.
1800	Germany	*The Jew in the Bush*, a story from the German Grimm's Fairy Tales, has as its main character a cheating, thieving Jew who winds up on the gallows. Even nursery rhymes turned out to be Anti-Semitic.

Date	Place	Description
1844	Germany	Karl Marx published *Zur Judenfrage* (On the Jewish Question), an economic and cultural criticism of Jews and Judaism.
1855	Germany	**Comte de Gobineau published his *Essay on Inequality*, which held that human races were unequal, the Nordic race being most superior. Nazi Anti-Semitism drew heavily from this racist thesis.**
1871	Czech Republic	Der Talmudjude, *The Talmud Jew*, was published. This vicious Anti-Semitic pamphlet was written by Father August Rohling of Prague, one of the founders of modern Anti-Semitism. It was widely reprinted and circulated in the Catholic press.
1880	Germany	By the end of 1880, the dominant theme of public affairs in Berlin was Anti-Semitism. A whole publishing industry developed to feed it. Anti-Semitic leaflets and libels against everything Jewish or suspected of Jewish sympathies were spread on a large scale.
1881	Germany	German Social Scientist and Philosopher, Eugen Dühring, published *The Jewish Question as a Problem of Race, Customs and Culture*. In this book he slandered the Jews as an intellectually inferior and depraved race who lack loyalty, reverence and any scientific and artistic creativity. **He declared that it was the duty of Nordic people to exterminate such a parasitic race as we**

PART 2 – AN OUTLINE OF THE HISTORY OF "CHRISTIAN" ANTI-SEMITISM

Date	Place	Description
		exterminate snakes and beasts of prey.
1887	Austria	In Vienna, Karl Lueger made his public conversion to Anti-Semitism. He became the Anti-Semitic Lord Mayor of Vienna and a major leader in Austrian Anti-Semitism. **In *Mein Kampf*, Hitler attributes his Anti-Semitism to the influence of Lueger.**
1888	New York	*An American Jew*, a viciously Anti-Semitic book, was published anonymously in New York City.
1889	Hungary	In Pressburg, the first Hungarian Anti-Semitic newspaper began publication.
1924	America	A KKK book entitled *Christ and Other Klansmen* was published. It purported that Jesus Christ embodied the true ideal of the Klan and should be counted as its first real member. It blamed the Jews for the death of Christ and stated that God was the real founder of the KKK.
1937	Germany	Nazi propaganda actively and directly incited popular Anti-Semitism. *Der Sturmer*, a Nazi newspaper, provided graphic documentation of the sadistic element of Anti-Semitism. It regularly devoted issues to the theme of ritual murder which was illustrated in gory detail.

9) Mandatory Conversion

The message of the Church was not the Biblical message of Salvation. **Jews were confronted with this demonically inspired ultimatum: Convert, leave or die.** If you did not submit to baptism, you and your family faced expulsion, torture or death. Forced baptism meant that you had to renounce and reject everything about being a Jew. You had to deny and abandon your family, your people, your culture, your Bible, your religion and your God. To save your, and your family's life, you were forced to reject your true identity and take on the false identity of a "Christian." This *conversion* and its required baptism meant that you became one with the *religion* of the haters, persecutors and the murderers of your own people.

It is only demonic spirits that could motivate Church leaders to tell the Jews, **"Become a 'Christian' or we will expel, torture or kill you."** Hatred, persecution and death are the fruits of all doctrines of demons. Remember all of this was done in the *Name of Jesus – the Prince of Peace*. This is why the words *baptism* and *conversion* are such profoundly negative words to Jewish people.

Authentic Biblical baptism signifies a true Scriptural conversion which is a supernatural change of heart and life. To real *born again* believers, *conversion* is a wonderful word. It means that you have been brought from darkness to light, from sin to salvation, from Satan to God. In this sense, the word *conversion* represents one of the most glorious spiritual experiences anyone can ever have.

These incidents took place in the years: 351, 418, 440, 457, 554, 582, 612, 629, 653, 655, 681, 722, 1012, 1096, 1191, 1215, 1279, 1290, 1320, 1349, 1389, 1391, 1392, 1414, 1415, 1453, 1563, 1577, 1578, 1593, 1630, 1637, 1655, 1775, 1793, 1823, 1827 and 1850.

Date	**Place**	**Description**
351	Roman Empire	Ursicinus, a Roman Legate, required Jews to violate the Sabbath and Passover during the military campaign

PART 2 – AN OUTLINE OF THE HISTORY OF "CHRISTIAN" ANTI-SEMITISM

Date	**Place**	**Description**
		against Persia.
582	Merovingia	Merovingian King Chilperic ordered all Jews to convert to Christianity or have their eyes torn out.
629	Merovingia	Merovingian King Dagobert ordered the forced conversion of Jews in his kingdom. Those who refused to convert would be treated as enemies and put to death.
722	Byzantium	Byzantine Emperor Leo III outlawed Judaism and required all Jews to be baptized. Some converted, but others burned to death in their synagogues to avoid baptism.
1191	France	The French King Philip surrounded the town of Bray and gave Jews the choice of baptism or death. The community decided on suicide, but Philip still had 100 burned. Children under 13 were spared.
1263	Spain	Pablo Christiani a Jewish convert to Catholicism led a *public disputation* with the famous Rabbi Nachmanides, known by his acronym "Ramban." The king was so impressed with the "Ramban" that he gave him 300 gold coins and declared that he had never heard "an unjust cause so nobly defended." However, church leaders banished him from Spain and he fled to Jerusalem. This event began a three century long process of rigged "debates" which would only bring various

Date	Place	Description
		disasters upon the Jewish people.
1389	Czech Republic	In Prague, thousands of Jews were murdered and many committed suicide to avoid forced baptism.
1391	Spain	In Castile, the synagogues were converted into churches and the Jewish quarter was destroyed. Those not forcibly converted were either slaughtered or sold as slaves to Muslims. In Valencia, close to 250 members of the Jewish community were murdered. The rest were forcibly converted. In Barcelona, a Christian mob attacked the Jewish community and 300 Jews were killed or committed suicide. There were 11,000 who were forcibly baptized. The preaching of the famous Dominican priest, Vicente Ferrer, helped to inspire the expulsion of the Jewish people who refused to convert.
1414	Spain	In Aragon, forced conversions were carried out. Jews who refused baptism were arrested. Whole communities were destroyed.
1563	Russia	Ivan the Terrible viewed Jews as evil influences and corrupters of Christians. When Russian troops occupied the Polish border city of Polotzk, the Czar gave orders that all local Jews were to be converted to the Greek Orthodox

PART 2 – AN OUTLINE OF THE HISTORY OF "CHRISTIAN" ANTI-SEMITISM

Date	Place	Description
		faith. Those who refused baptism were drowned in the Dvina River.
1578	Rome	Pope Gregory XIII required the Jews of Rome to maintain a *house of conversion*.[50]
1593	Berlin	Jews were given the choice of baptism or expulsion.
1827	Russia	There were many accounts of torture and beatings with the aim of converting the Jews to Russian Orthodoxy. The conversion rate was high and suicide was frequent.

10) Imprisonment, Torture and Slavery

These incidents took place in the years: 1336, 1349, 1368, 1450, 1492, 1453, 1555, 1596, 1648, 1655 and 1702.

Date	Place	Description
1336	Spain	Alfonso XI imprisoned and tortured high court Jews. Many died as a result.
1368	Spain	In Granada, Pedro "the Cruel" permitted his Moslem allies to sell 300 Jewish families from Jaén into slavery.
1450	Germany	All Jews in Bavaria were arrested. The men were thrown into prison and the women were locked in the synagogues while their possessions were stolen. Then they were all expelled.
1453	Poland	In Breslau, following the preaching of

---

[50] A place where *converted* Jews were sent to live.

Date	Place	Description
		Godfrey, Bishop and Duke of Franconia, the Jewish community, men, women and children were imprisoned, and their property and lands were confiscated.
1648	Ukraine	Jews in Kiev fled to the Tartar camps and surrendered. As a rule, the Tartars refrained from killing them. Instead, they sold them into slavery in Turkey, where there was an excellent chance of their being purchased by Turkish Jews.

11) Murder and Slaughter of Individual Jews

These incidents took place in the years: 1147, 1321, 1349, 1366, 1391, 1399, 1400, 1449, 1463, 1481, 1484, 1485, 1486, 1488, 1490, 1539, 1556, 1564, 1637, 1647, 1652, 1655, 1663, 1738 and 1753.

Date	Place	Description
1147	Germany	In Würzburg, twenty members of the Jewish community were murdered by Crusaders because of a rumor that they had murdered a Christian.
		In Belitz, all Jews were burned on the basis of a ritual murder charge.
1147	Czech Republic	In Bohemia, the Crusaders murdered 150 Jews.
1321	Spain	Two Jews in the village of Teruel were accused of poisoning a well and were executed.
1391	Spain	In Toledo, Rabbi Judah's family and his students were slaughtered.

PART 2 – AN OUTLINE OF THE HISTORY OF "CHRISTIAN" ANTI-SEMITISM

Date	**Place**	**Description**
		In Madrid, those of the community who did not convert were slaughtered. The same fate befell the congregations of Seville, Cordova and Barcelona. In Seville, 4,000 Jews were murdered, and the women and children were sold as slaves to Arabs.
1400	Czech Republic	In Prague, a Jewish convert to "Christianity" named Pessach-Peter charged 80 Jews with making blasphemous statements and Anti-Christian prayers. These Jews were arrested and burned at the stake.
1463	Poland	On route to the Crusade against the Turks, Polish troops attacked the Jews in Krakow, looted their homes and killed about 30 people.
1484	Spain	In Villareal, 34 Jews were burned alive. In Guadalupe, 52 Conversos, Jews who had converted to Christianity and were a special target of the Inquisition, were burned at the stake for continuing to secretly practice Judaism. More than 45 Conversos' corpses were exhumed from their graves and burned at the stake and 25 Conversos who had fled were burned in effigy. In Saragossa, two Conversos were burned alive. A woman's corpse was exhumed and burned. About 30 Conversos in Teruel were sent to the stake.

Date	Place	Description
1488	Spain	In Toledo, 40 Conversos were burned.
1539	Poland	In Krakow, Catherine Zaleshouska, a Catholic and the wife of an official, was convicted of denying the fundamental dogmas of Christianity and adhering secretly to Jewish doctrines. Failing to bring her back to the Church, Peter Gamrut, the Bishop, condemned her to death. She was burned at the stake in the market place.
1556	Poland	In Sokhachev, a woman was accused of selling the *Holy Wafer* she had received during communion to three Jews. The Jews and this woman were accused of stabbing the wafer until it bled. On the order of the Bishop of Chelm, they were all tortured on the rack and then burned at the stake.
1647	Portugal	The Marrano Isaac de Castro Tortos, a Dutch citizen, was burned by the Inquisition in Lisbon.
1652	Portugal	Manuel Fernando de Villareal, a Marrano who conducted diplomatic affairs, was burned at the stake.
1655	Spain	A Marrano youth was burned at the stake in Granada.
		In Cordoba, Abraham Nunez Bernal, a Marrano, was burned.
1663	Poland	In Krakow, Mattathiah Calabona, a Jew, argued with a local priest about religious topics. Charges of blasphemy were

PART 2 – AN OUTLINE OF THE HISTORY OF "CHRISTIAN" ANTI-SEMITISM

Date	Place	Description
		brought against him. He pleaded innocent and claimed ignorance of German. He refused to confess even after being tortured. He was sentenced to death. His execution was carried out in the following manner: first his lips were cut off, next his hand, then his tongue. He was burned at the stake, and the ashes were shot into the air from a cannon.
1738	Russia	Borukh Liebov, after being banished by Catherine I, continued to travel into Russia. He converted a retired naval captain, and when he was circumcised, his conversion became known. Both were then arrested, and after prolonged torture they were burned alive on July 15.
1753	Poland	Twenty-four Jews were arrested in Zlytrovia for the murder of a peasant boy named Studzienski. Under torture, they confessed. Of the group 11 were skinned alive and 13 accepted baptism to avoid execution.

12) Execution of Parents and Separation of Children from Parents

Incidents that took place in the years: 469, 470, 633, 693, 694, 1407, 1422, 1453, 1492, 1497, 1747 and 1858.

Date	Place	Description
469-470	Persia	Emperor Firiz executed half the Jewish population of Ipahan after Jews were accused of murdering two men. Jewish children were taken from their families

Date	Place	Description
		and raised in a temple dedicated to the Persian fire god.
633	Spain	The Third Council of Toledo decreed that all Jewish children of both sexes were to be forcibly taken from their parents and raised in monasteries.
693	Spain	In Toledo, the Seventeenth Council declared all Jews slaves, confiscated their property and turned it over to former Christian slaves. Jewish children were forcibly removed from parental control and were raised in Christian houses or monasteries. They were later to be married to persons of non-Jewish descent.
1407	Poland	In Krakow, during the Easter season, a priest named Budek charged that the Jews had killed a Christian boy and mocked his blood and had thrown stones at a priest with a crucifix in his hands. A mob began looting the Jewish quarter. Many houses were set on fire. Survivors who did not convert were slaughtered and the children of victims were baptized.
1422	Austria	Archduke Albert ordered all Jews in the realm arrested. Poorer Jews were banished while the wealthier were imprisoned. Their property was confiscated and the children were taken and raised as Christians.
1497	Portugal	King Manuel issued a secret command that all Jewish children under the age of

PART 2 – AN OUTLINE OF THE HISTORY OF "CHRISTIAN" ANTI-SEMITISM

Date	Place	Description
		14 were to be taken from their parents and baptized on Easter Sunday.
1747	Rome	Pope Benedict XIV issued a papal bull asserting that all Jewish children over the age of 7 could be baptized against the will of their parents.

13) Mob Attacks and Riots

These incidents took place in the years: 1370, 1454, 1506, 1577, 1592, 1614, 1635, 1637, 1648, 1663, 1664, 1670, 1671, 1681, 1682, 1734, 1750, 1768, 1789, 1801, 1819, 1821, 1848, 1850, 1855, 1866, 1871, 1881, 1887, 1897, 1898, 1904, 1905, 1919, 1920, 1928, 1930, 1933 and 1936.

Date	Place	Description
1506	Portugal	In Lisbon, a mob stirred by the preaching of Dominicans murdered between 2,000 and 4,000 Conversos. Men, women and children were victims. Women and children were thrown from windows and caught on the spears of street mobs. The slaughter was accompanied by widespread rape of women and girls.
1592	Poland	In Vilna, the synagogue and Jewish homes were destroyed. In Posen, mobs attacked the Jewish quarter on a regular basis.
1614	Germany	The Jewish community in Frankfurt was destroyed and 2,920 Jews were murdered.
1635	Poland	In Vilna, an Anti-Jewish riot took place.

Date	Place	Description
1637	Poland	Because a Pole was convicted of having stolen some church vessels, the Jewish quarter in Krakow was attacked by mobs. Forty Jews from the ghetto were taken to the river. Thirty-three saved themselves by accepting baptism; the other seven were drowned.
		Cossacks and peasants attacked the Jewish community in Lubny. Several synagogues there and in surrounding towns were destroyed. About 200 Jews were killed.
1670	Poland	Laws were passed restricting Jewish trade and interactions with Christians. Street attacks on Jews by Christian college students became everyday events in the cities of Poland. These attacks involved not only insults and assaults on Jewish passers-by on the street, but also invasions of the Jewish quarter where robbery and violence were common occurrences.
1671	Belarus	In Minsk, the Jewish community was attacked by a mob.
1682	Poland	In Krakow, the Jewish community was attacked by a band of students and local residents.
1789	France	In Alsace, mobs attacked the Jews and destroyed houses and property. They were then forced to flee half naked from the province.
1801	Romania	A mob killed 128 Jews and destroyed

PART 2 – AN OUTLINE OF THE HISTORY OF "CHRISTIAN" ANTI-SEMITISM

Date	Place	Description
		most of the Jewish quarter in Bucharest.
1819	Germany	Anti-Jewish riots occurred in many cities in Germany.
1819	Denmark	Riots spread in Copenhagen and mobs attacked Jewish homes.
1848	Austria	The revolution served as a cover for mob attacks on Jewish property in Pressburg and Pest. A synagogue in Steinamanger was vandalized. The Torah scrolls were torn and thrown into the river.
1866	Romania	In Bucharest, a mob gathered to prevent the granting of equal citizenship to Jews. Synagogues, Torah scrolls and Holy books were desecrated and destroyed.
1882	Slovakia	In many towns, Anti-Semitic riots occurred and Jewish communities were attacked by mobs.
1919	Czech Republic	In Prague, a series of Anti-Jewish riots occurred. Jewish stores and factories were looted and vandalized.
1920	Germany & Poland	Anti-Jewish riots occurred in Munich and Breslau.
1928	Hungary	Anti-Jewish riots occurred in most Hungarian universities.
1928	Lithuania	The towns of Wilkowishki and Newl had violent Anti-Semitic riots.

Date	Place	Description
1930	Germany	On New Year's Day in Berlin, 8 Jews were killed in an Anti-Jewish riot. Jewish shops and homes were vandalized, and many Jews were beaten.
		Anti-Jewish riots occurred throughout the country following elections in September. Jews were beaten and Jewish homes and shops were vandalized in Wurzburg, Leipzig, Dusseldorf, Frankfurt and Berlin.
1930	Mexico	Anti-Jewish riots occurred in the Lagunilla Market in Mexico City.
1936	Poland	In April there were widespread riots in Poland and Galicia. 79 Jews were killed and over 500 were wounded.
1936	Romania	In Bucharest, the largest Anti-Semitic march in Romanian history involving approximately 210,000 participants took place. Anti-Jewish riots occurred in all major Romanian cities.

14) Jewish Communities and Quarters Attacked and Burned

These incidents took place in the years: 489, 506, 554, 1063, 1096, 1099, 1100, 1140, 1146, 1147, 1171, 1188, 1190, 1209, 1236, 1239, 1244, 1261, 1262, 1264, 1270, 1298, 1320, 1328, 1348, 1349, 1366, 1380, 1381, 1384, 1414, 1422, 1559, 1648, 1649, 1656, 1687, 1689, 1768 and 1850.

Date	Place	Description
489	Antioch	The Jewish quarter in Antioch was attacked by a Christian mob. The

PART 2 – AN OUTLINE OF THE HISTORY OF "CHRISTIAN" ANTI-SEMITISM

Date	Place	Description
		synagogue was burned and the bodies of slain Jews were thrown into a fire. Emperor Zeno asked why live Jews were not burned as well.
1099	Jerusalem	**Godfrey of Bouillon, a Crusader wearing a cross, took Jerusalem. He massacred the Muslims and drove the Jews into a synagogue and set it on fire. While men, women and children were screaming as they were being burned alive, the Crusaders were singing, "Our Lord Jesus Christ, we adore you."** **This was one of the most *Scarring* events in Jewish history and it is often singled out as representative of all other "Christian" Anti-Semitic persecution.**
1140	Germany	Massacres occurred in Cologne, Mainz, Worms, Speyer and Strasburg.
1146	Germany	The preaching of the monk, Radolph, encouraged mob attacks, forced baptisms and massacres of Jews in Mayence, Cologne and other communities in the Rhine Valley.
1147	Germany	Twenty members of the Jewish community of Wurzburg were murdered by Crusaders because of a rumor that they had murdered a Christian.
1147	Czech Republic	In Bohemia, 150 Jews were murdered by Crusaders.

Date	Place	Description
1147	France	The communities of Carenton, Ramenu and Sully were attacked by Crusaders.
1236	France	Crusaders attacked the Jewish communities of: Anjou, Poitou, Bordeaux and Angouleme. Jews were given the choice of baptism or death. Five hundred chose baptism but more than 3,000 were brutally murdered, including children and pregnant women. Many were trampled to death by Crusaders' horses.
1261	England	Students, with priests and monks participating, attacked the Jewish quarter in Canterbury.
1262	London	Anti-Jewish riots occurred. The Jewish quarter was sacked.
1349	Switzerland	In January, the Jewish community of Basle was burned to death in a house especially constructed for that purpose. This house was located on an island in the Rhine.
1381	France	Mobs attacked, plundered and murdered Jews in Paris and other provinces in France during the Maillotin uprising.
1559	Czech Republic	In Prague, a fire in the Jewish quarter destroyed many houses. A "Christian" mob roamed into the section and threw many women and children into the flames as they plundered the quarter.
1649	Poland	Peace negotiations were being conducted between the Cossacks and the new

PART 2 – AN OUTLINE OF THE HISTORY OF "CHRISTIAN" ANTI-SEMITISM

Date	Place	Description
		Polish King, John Casimir. Civil war broke out once again in the spring. As a result, many more Jewish communities were destroyed by the Cossacks.
1687	Poland	"Christian" students in Posen attacked the Jewish quarter. A fierce battle lasted for 3 days.

15) Wearing of Badges or Distinctive Dress to Identify Jews

These incidents took place in the years: 1215, 1218, 1275, 1279, 1313, 1392, 1434, 1443, 1451, 1457, 1540, 1542, 1555, 1797 and 1937.

During the time of the Crusades, 1000 through 1348, the Fourth Lateran Council decreed that all Jews make themselves visible by requiring them to wear the *Jew badge*.

Date	Place	Description
1218	England	King Henry III issued a royal decree requiring all Jews in England to wear a badge on their outer garments at all times so that they could be distinguished from Christians.
1412	Spain	In Castile and Aragon, legislation was passed specifying dress and hair styles for Jews. The use of Christian names was forbidden.
1434	Germany	In Augsburg, Jews were required to wear a yellow wheel on their clothing.
1443	Italy	In Venice, Jews were required to wear a yellow badge.

Date	Place	Description
1451	Germany	The Catholic Cardinal, Nicholas de Cusa, required the Jewish men to wear round pieces of red cloth on their chests and women to wear blue strips on their headdresses.
1457	Germany	The Archbishop of Mayence required all Jews to wear distinctive markings on their clothing.
1540	Italy	In Naples, Charles V ordered Jews to wear a badge or leave the city. They chose voluntary exile.
1797	Italy	In Rome, Jews were required to wear distinctive badges on their clothing.
1939	Poland	Just after the Nazi invasion of Poland all Jews older than ten were to wear a white badge with a Star of David on their right arm. Two years later, on September 1, 1941, it was decreed that all Jews within Germany as well as in all occupied territories were to wear a yellow Star of David with the word *Jude* (Jew) on the left side of one's chest.

16) Expulsion of Jews

These incidents took place in the years: 250, 258, 325, 415, 628, 638, 642, 855, 876, 1181, 1290, 1306, 1311, 1348, 1349, 1388, 1394, 1420, 1422, 1424, 1426, 1432, 1438, 1439, 1440, 1453, 1454, 1480, 1483, 1485, 1492, 1495, 1497, 1498, 1499, 1514, 1519, 1537, 1540, 1542, 1550, 1551, 1558, 1559, 1561, 1567, 1571, 1582, 1593, 1597, 1615, 1619, 1649, 1654, 1656, 1655, 1669, 1685, 1699, 1712, 1727, 1738, 1739, 1740, 1741, 1744, 1745, 1753, 1761, 1775, 1783,

PART 2 – AN OUTLINE OF THE HISTORY OF "CHRISTIAN" ANTI-SEMITISM

1808, 1815, 1819, 1820, 1824, 1825, 1829, 1866, 1900, 1922 and 1937.

As can be noted from the dates referenced above, recorded expulsions of the Jews from areas or countries began as early as 250 years after Christ.

Date	Place	Description
1290	England	All Jews expelled.
1306 & 1394	France	All Jews expelled.
1349 & 1360	Hungary	All Jews expelled.
1492	Spain	All Jews expelled.
1497	Portugal	All Jews expelled.
1593	Italy	All Jews expelled.
1593	Bavaria	All Jews expelled.
1808	Russia	The Czar issued an edict for the expulsion of Jews from the villages and from the countryside. The expulsion was to be spread over a 3-year period. Approximately 500,000 Jews were displaced. However, the edict was cancelled late in 1808 for fear of an epidemic spreading.
1815	Germany	Jewish families were forced to leave Lubeck and Bremen. Germany's decline and occupation by foreign troops was blamed on Jewish prosperity.

Date	Place	Description
1937	Italy	In September, the Italian government ordered all foreign Jews and those who had acquired citizenship since 1919 to leave the country within 6 months.

17) Mass Extermination of Jews

These incidents took place in the years: 113, 116, 132, 506, 1096, 1099, 1140, 1146, 1190, 1209, 1270, 1298, 1320, 1328, 1338, 1348, 1349, 1354, 1366, 1391, 1407, 1422, 1473, 1506, 1648, 1654, 1656, 1657, 1664, 1689, 1734, 1750, 1768, 1772, 1919, 1938, 1939, 1940, 1941, 1942, 1943 and 1944.

Depending upon the historic period referred to, attempted annihilation of the Jewish people has been referred to by such terms as *massacre*, *elimination*, *slaughter* and *extermination*. As can be noted from the dates above, rather than being a phenomenon of one historical period known as *the Holocaust*, Satan's goal has remained consistent.

Date	Place	Description
1095	France & Germany	Instigated by Pope Urban II the First Crusade was launched. Although the prime goal of the Crusades was to liberate Jerusalem from the Muslims, Jews were a second target. Inspired by preachers such as Peter the Hermit, who promised eternal salvation to those who killed the Jews, the soldiers marched through Europe challenging every Jew with these frightful words, **"Christ-killers, embrace the Cross or die!"** Untold numbers were forced into baptism or were killed. In the Rhine Valley alone 12,000 Jews were killed. This represented between one-third and one-fourth of the Jewish population. This murderous behavior continued until

PART 2 – AN OUTLINE OF THE HISTORY OF "CHRISTIAN" ANTI-SEMITISM

Date	Place	Description
		the ninth crusade in 1272.
1140	Germany	Massacres occurred in Cologne, Mainz, Worms, Speyer and Strasburg.
1190	England	Crusaders attack the Jewish community in York. Besieged by the mob, 150 Jews took refuge in Clifford's tower. Faced with forced conversion, they chose suicide. Fathers killed their wives and children and then each other.
1270	Germany	Massacres of Jewish communities occurred in Erfurt, Weissenberg, Magdeburg, Arnstadt and Coblenz. In Sinzig, the Jews were locked in the synagogue and burned alive.
1298	Germany	Responding to a rumor of Host Desecration, Rindfleisch, a German nobleman, put together a small army called the *Judenschachter* (Jew slaughterers) and for about six months massacred more than 140 Jewish communities. The entire Jewish population of Rottingen was burned alive. An estimated 100,000 Jews were slain.
1328	Spain	In Estella, 5,000 Jews were massacred when a "Christian" mob, inflamed by the Anti-Jewish preaching of a traveling friar, attacked the Jewish community.
1349	Switzerland	The Jewish community of Basle burned to death in a house especially constructed for that purpose.
1349	Germany	At approximately the same time, all

Date	Place	Description
		Jews in Freiburg were burned at the stake, except for 12 men who were permitted to live in order to discover the names of their creditors.
		In Mayence, there were 6,000 Jews burned to death when a mob attacked the community and burned their houses.
		In Erfurt, more than 3,000 Jews were slaughtered, virtually the entire community.
		The communities of Augsburg, Wurzburg and Swabia Munich were destroyed.
		Margrave Louis of Brandenburg ordered all Jews burned and their property confiscated.
1349	Austria	The entire Jewish community of Strasburg was imprisoned. The following Sabbath they were dragged to the burial ground and burned at the stake. Two thousand perished.
1349	Poland	In Breslau, the entire Jewish community was completely exterminated.
1349	Belgium	A mob attacked the Jewish community in Brussels and approximately 500 people were massacred.
1384	Germany	In Nordlingen, a mob spurred on by clergy attacked and murdered every Jewish man, woman and child.

PART 2 – AN OUTLINE OF THE HISTORY OF "CHRISTIAN" ANTI-SEMITISM

Date	**Place**	**Description**
1648-1649	Poland & Ukraine	**The Cossack leader Bogdan (Khmelnitski) Chmielnicki led an uprising of Ukrainians against Polish rulers. His horrific massacres of the Jews is called the "gezerot tah ve-tat" – the "Abyss of Despair." It is impossible to determine accurately the number of victims who perished, but some Jewish sources say at least 100,000 were murdered and over 300 communities destroyed.** **The brutality of these massacres defies description. The killing of the Jews was accomplished by barbarous tortures: victims flayed alive, split asunder, club-bed to death, roasted on coals and scalded with boiling water. Even infants at the breast were not spared. The most terrible cruelty was shown toward the Jews. They were destined to utter annihilation and the slightest pity shown them was looked upon as treason.**
1657	Poland	The extent of the tragedy for Polish Jews during the decade 1648-1658 was incredible. Contemporary chroniclers numbered Jewish victims of the massacres at between 100,000 and 500,000. Some 700 communities in Poland were pillaged and the people were massacred.
1657	Ukraine	In the Ukrainian cities on the left bank of the Dnieper, the region of the Cossacks, the provinces of Chernigov, Poltava and Kiev, the Jewish communities almost completely disappeared.

Date	Place	Description
		On the right side of the Dnieper, in Volhynia, Podolia and the Polish Ukraine, only about 1/10 of the Jewish population survived.
1689	Germany	The Jewish community in Worms was massacred.
1734	Ukraine	Cossack commanders organized armies to devastate many Jewish villages in the provinces of Kiev, Volhynia and Podolia. The brutality of the slaughters matched those of the 17th century.
1768	Ukraine	In Uman, Jews were murdered in Cossack fashion: women were first raped before being trampled to death by horses. A crowd of 3,000 was slaughtered one by one in the synagogue. While the Uman massacre was taking place, smaller detachments of rebels were exterminating the Jews in other parts of the Ukraine.
1919	Ukraine	More than 493 pogroms (government sponsored massacres), resulted in the murders of more than 70,000 Jews.

Instances of Aid to the Jews

Throughout the history of Anti-Semitism, there have been attempts to protect the Jewish people. Though such incidents have been sporadic and for the most part insignificant in the overall picture of the persecution of the Jewish people, it is important to realize that no matter how severe the persecution and the penalties for aiding the Jews, there have been people who did. There are many heroic accounts of those who came to the aid of the Jews during the

PART 2 – AN OUTLINE OF THE HISTORY OF "CHRISTIAN" ANTI-SEMITISM

Holocaust, and I will not attempt to retell those testimonies here. Their names are enshrined forever with trees planted in their honor on the *Avenue of the Righteous* at Yad Vashem, Israel's official memorial to the victims of the Holocaust in Jerusalem. I will simply set forth several instances illustrating this aspect of our study.

Date	Place	Description
138	Rome	The successor to Hadrian, Antoninus Pius, restored Jewish religious freedom. However, in order to limit the spread of Judaism and stop Jewish proselytizing, he retained the restrictions against circumcising non-Jews under pain of death or banishment.
379	Rome	Emperor Theodosius the Great protected Jews from the Church's persecution of heretics. He did however permit the destruction of synagogues if it served a religious purpose. Christianity became the state religion of the Roman Empire at this time.
590	Rome	Pope Gregory I, also known as "Gregory the Great," declared that Christians were required to protect and defend the Jewish people. He outlawed acts of violence and persecution of the Jews. He rejected the use of forced baptism, and protected both the civil and religious rights of the Jews.
1120	Rome	Calixtus II issued the papal bull "Sicut Judaeis" (Latin: "As the Jews"). Prompted by the slaughter of over 5,000 Jews during the First Crusade, it forbade, on pain of excommunication, forced conversions, physical violence, confiscation of property or disturbing the Jews relig-

Date	Place	Description

ious observances. It stated that Jews were entitled to "enjoy their lawful liberty."

"Sicut Judaeis" was later reaffirmed by popes Alexander III, Celestine III (1191-1198), Innocent III (1199), Honorius III (1216), Gregory IX (1235), Innocent IV (1246), Alexander IV (1255), Urban IV (1262), Gregory X (1272 & 1274), Nicholas III, Martin IV (1281), Honorius IV (1285-1287), Nicholas IV (1288–92), Clement VI (1348), Urban V (1365), Boniface IX (1389), Martin V (1422), and Nicholas V (1447).

1144	Germany	The preaching of the Cistercian monk, Bernard of Clairvaux, in Mainz, stopped crusaders from slaughtering Jews. Remembered by Jews of that area as a "righteous gentile," many named their children Bernard (ex. Bernard Baruch). He taught that the Church should try to convince and convert the Jews, but they must not be persecuted, slaughtered, nor even driven out.
1188	England	The coronation of Richard I was followed by mob attacks on the Jewish communities of London and York. Richard punished the rioters and permitted those who had converted to avoid death by returning to their faith.
1235	Germany	Emperor Frederick II had several Jewish scholars at his court. When the Jews of Fulda were accused of "ritual murder,"

PART 2 – AN OUTLINE OF THE HISTORY OF "CHRISTIAN" ANTI-SEMITISM

Date	Place	Description
		Frederick came to their rescue and denounced the story as a cruel legend.
1247	Rome	Pope Innocent IV conducted an investigation of widespread ritual murder libel and completely exonerated Jews of the charge.
1264	Poland	Bolesław the Pious, King of Poland, issued the Statute of Kalisz. This granted Jews the same protections as Christians. Jews were free to worship and work and were secure in their possessions.
1273	Rome	Pope Gregory X issued "an encyclical to all Christians forbidding them to baptize Jews by force or to injure their persons or to take away their money or to disturb them during the celebration of their religious festivals."
1275	England	King Edward I passed the *Statutum Judeismo*. Although this law put various restrictions on them, for the first time Jews were allowed to lease land for farming and were granted the right to become merchants and artisans.
1334	Poland	King Casimir the 3rd extended the rights and protections granted by the Statute of Kalisz. This opened doors for Jews to flee the persecutions in other European nations and find safety and freedom in Poland.
1348	Rome	Clement VI issued a papal bull which declared the Jews innocent of the charge

Date	Place	Description
		of causing the plague and attempted to show the absurdity of the charge. He admonished the clergy to give protection to the Jews and excommunicated accusers and murderers.
1348	France	In Strasbourg, community leaders made great efforts to prove Jews innocent and defended them against mob attacks and the Bishop's demand for extermination. The authorities of Basle, Freiburg and Cologne followed similar courses.
1419	Rome	Pope Martin V and the Spanish kings abolished a series of earlier Anti-Jewish laws. The Talmud and synagogues were returned to the Jews and Anti-Jewish laws were not enforced.
1447	Poland	King Casimir IV renewed and confirmed the old privileges for the Jewish people and also granted new ones, such as the Jews of Poland had never before enjoyed. He decreed that any Christian who brought the charge of ritual murder against Jews and could not prove it conclusively was to be put to death.
1562	Rome	Pope Pius IV suspended many of the Anti-Jewish edicts of Pope Paul IV.
1616	Germany	Jews were readmitted to Worms. The Jews of Frankfurt were led back to the city in triumphant procession. The city was fined 175,919 florins by the emperor as compensation for the losses suffered by the Jews.

PART 2 – AN OUTLINE OF THE HISTORY OF "CHRISTIAN" ANTI-SEMITISM

Date	Place	Description
1620	America	The Jews experience freedom in the New World.
1656	England	Under the protectorate of Oliver Cromwell, the Jews were readmitted to England after they were expelled in 1290 by King Edward I.
1698	England	For the first time, the practice of Judaism received parliamentary sanction in addition to royal protection.
1791	France	The French National Assembly repealed all Anti-Jewish laws and in November, Louis XVI proclaimed full equality for the Jews.
1940	Denmark	Throughout the German occupation, King Christian and the majority of the Danish people, stood by their Jewish citizens and were instrumental in saving almost all of them from Nazi persecution and death.
1940	Netherlands	Devout Christian, Corrie ten Boom, and her family, helped Jews escape the Nazi Holocaust during World War II and, by all accounts, saved nearly 800 lives.
1940	Warsaw Ghetto	Polish nurse, Irena Sendler, rescued 2500 Jewish children and also distributed more than 3,000 false documents to help Jews escape.

Corrie ten Boom and Irena Sendler are just two examples of many who risked and gave their lives to save Jews during the Holocaust (see: http://www.yadvashem.org/yv/en/righteous/index.asp).

The Holocaust 1933-1945

There may be no more succinct description of the Holocaust than the statement issued by the Vatican on March 12, 1998: "This century has witnessed an unspeakable tragedy, which can never be forgotten — the attempt by the Nazi regime to exterminate the Jewish people, with the consequent killing of millions of Jews. Women and men, old and young, children and infants, for the sole reason of their Jewish origin, were persecuted and deported. Some were killed immediately, while others were degraded, ill-treated, tortured and utterly robbed of their human dignity, and then murdered. Very few of those who entered the [concentration] camps survived, and those who did remained scarred for life. This was the Holocaust."

Because the Holocaust is the defining and most scarring event of the modern Jewish world, I want to present it to you with some specific details to help you understand its horrors.

The Holocaust differed from other periods of Anti-Semitic violence, such as during the Crusades and Pogroms, in that there was no haven and virtually no escape for Jews under Nazi control. The actual survival of the Jews of Europe was never more seriously threatened than it was during this period. If the Nazis had won World War II, there is no doubt that Satan would have succeeded in reaching his goal of exterminating all the Jews in Europe. Of course he wouldn't have stopped there!

As we view the present opposition to the nation of Israel through the lens of history, we recognize that opposition for what it is: the attempt to annihilate God's Covenant people from the earth, thus preventing God's Word from coming to pass and His theocratic rule from being inaugurated through the King of the Jews, Yeshua (Jesus) the Messiah.

PART 2 – AN OUTLINE OF THE HISTORY OF "CHRISTIAN" ANTI-SEMITISM

Holocaust Statistics

(All numbers estimates*)
(Chart from: http://history1900s.about.com/library/holocaust/bldied.htm)

Country	Pre-war Jewish Population	Estimated Murdered
Austria	185,000	50,000
Belgium	66,000	25,000
Bohemia/Moravia	118,000	78,000
Bulgaria	50,000	0
Denmark	8,000	60
Estonia	4,500	2,000
Finland	2,000	7
France	350,000	77,000
Germany	565,000	142,000
Greece	75,000	65,000
Hungary	825,000	550,000
Italy	44,500	7,500
Latvia	91,500	70,000
Lithuania	168,000	140,000
Luxembourg	3,500	1,000
Netherlands	140,000	100,000
Norway	1,700	762
Poland	3,300,000	3,000,000
Romania	609,000	270,000
Slovakia	89,000	71,000
Soviet Union	3,020,000	1,000,000
Yugoslavia	78,000	60,000
Total:	9,793,700	5,709,329

*For additional estimates see:

Lucy Dawidowicz, The War Against the Jews, 1933-1945 (New York: Bantam Books, 1986) 403.

Abraham and Hershel Edelheit, History of the Holocaust (Boulder: Westview Press, 1994) 266.

Israel Gutman (ed.), Encyclopedia of the Holocaust (New York: Macmillan Library Reference USA, 1990) 1799.

Raul Hilberg, Destruction of European Jews (New York: Holmes & Meier Publishers, 1985) 1220.

SO DEEPLY SCARRED

LOCATIONS OF EXTERMINATION CAMPS
https://upload.wikimedia.org/wikipedia/commons/thumb/d/d0/WW2-Holocaust-Poland.PNG/330px-WW2-Holocaust-Poland.PNG

Extermination Camps
Charts from: http://www.nationalww2museum.org/

Name	Country	Number of Deaths
Auschwitz-Birkenau	Poland	Over 1,000,000
Belzec	Poland	435,000
Chelmno	Poland	150,000
Majdanek	Poland	78,000
Sobibor	Poland	200,000
Treblinka	Poland	870,000

PART 2 – AN OUTLINE OF THE HISTORY OF "CHRISTIAN" ANTI-SEMITISM

Major Concentration Camps

Name	Country	Description
Dachau	Germany	200,000 held; 32,000 deaths; the first German concentration camp, established in 1933, soon after Hitler's rise to power
Buchenwald	Germany	250,000 held; 56,000 deaths; the largest concentration camp in Germany
Mauthausen	Austria	195,000 held; 95,000 deaths; included more than 50 sub-camps
Bergen-Belsen	Germany	70,000 deaths
Flossenberg	Germany	100,000 held; 30,000 deaths
Dora-Mittelbau	Germany	60,000 held; 20,000 deaths; provided slave labor for German V-2 rocket production
Gross-Rosen	Poland	125,000 held; 40,000 deaths; included up to 60 sub-camps
Ravensbruck	Germany	Camp for Women: 150,000 held; 90,000 deaths
Westerbork	Netherlands	102,000 Dutch Jews deported to extermination camps
Sachsenhausen	Germany	200,000 held; 100,000 deaths
Plaszow	Poland	150,000 held; 9,000 deaths; from here German industrialist Oscar Schindler saved 1,200 Jews
Drancy	France	70,000 French Jews deported to extermination camps

Name	Country	Description
Theresienstadt	Czech Republic	140,000 held; 35,000 deaths
Stutthof	Poland	110,000 held; 65,000 deaths; first concentration camp built by Germans outside Germany
Neuengamme	Germany	106,000 held; 43,000 deaths
Natzweiler-Struthof	France	40,000 held; 25,000 deaths; the only German-built concentration camp in France (Vichy France controlled others)
Jasenovac	Croatia today	100,000 held; 100,000 deaths

A Selected Overview of Holocaust Events

1925

Mein Kampf (My Struggle), by Adolph Hitler, is published. It includes these quotes:

> "Was there any form of filth or profligacy, particularly in cultural life, without at least one Jew involved in it?...Slowly I had become an expert in their own doctrine and used it as a weapon in the struggle for my own profound conviction. Success almost always favored my side. The great masses could be saved, if only with the gravest sacrifice in time and patience. But a Jew could never be parted from his opinions...I didn't know what to be more amazed at: the agility of their tongues or their virtuosity at lying.

PART 2 – AN OUTLINE OF THE HISTORY OF "CHRISTIAN" ANTI-SEMITISM

> **Gradually I began to hate them…If, with the help of the Marxist creed, the Jew is victorious over the other peoples of the world, his crown will be the funeral wreath of humanity…*Hence today I believe that I am acting in accordance with the will of the Almighty Creator. By defending myself against the Jew, I am fighting for the work of the Lord."***

1933

January 30, Hitler becomes Chancellor and immediately makes himself absolute ruler of Germany.

The Nazis begin a process of removing Jews from German public life. They boycott Jewish businesses by blocking the entrance to thousands of Jewish shops and painting a yellow Jewish *Star of David* across their doors and windows. They post signs telling people, "Don't Buy from Jews" and "The Jews Are Our Misfortune."

Jews are barred from civil service jobs, legal professions and universities. They are removed from all public offices. Jewish doctors are prohibited from treating German citizens. Jews are removed from editorial positions in all newspapers and forbidden to teach in schools.

1935

In Nuremberg, the Nazis announced a whole series of new laws which made Anti-Semitism the law of the land. The Jews lost their German citizenship, were denied the right to vote and were deprived of most social and political rights.

1936

In Germany, the Secret State Police (Gestapo) were granted the authority to operate without judicial review, putting them above the law. Essentially they became a law unto themselves. Their ability to detain and punish *enemies of the state* was unchallenged. It was said of the Gestapo that as long as they carried out the will of the leadership of the Nazi party they were acting *legally*. Their reign of terror began.

In Russia, Stalin began to purge all Jews from his government. Over the next few years many Jewish leaders were executed and Jewish schools and businesses were closed. There were Anti-Semitic riots in Poland, and the Polish Catholic Primate of Poland, Cardinal Hlond, urged Polish Catholics to boycott Jewish businesses. Events like these only served to embolden the Nazis.

1937

Nazi propaganda regularly enflamed Anti-Semitism in Germany. *Der Sturmer*, a major Nazi newspaper, fixated on various Anti-Semitic themes. Its illustrations caricatured the Jews in horrific ways.

The Sachsenhausen, Buchenwald and Lichtenburg concentration camps were established. The Gestapo ordered Jewish inmates to wear a yellow triangle to form a Star of David. The movement toward the removal of all Jews from German society and economy was increased.

1938

After the annexation of Austria, the SS set up a concentration camp at Mauthausen. In Vienna, Jewish men and women were forced to scrub street gutters, public latrines and the toilets of SA and SS barracks with toothbrushes.

The SS established the *Office for Jewish Emigration*. It became the sole agency for issuing permits for Jews to be able to leave the country. Headed by Reinhardt Heydrich and administrated by Adolph Eichmann, this office soon became the agency for the *extermination*, not emigration, of Jews.

All male Jews with criminal records were transferred to the Buchenwald concentration camp. All Jewish businesses were required to register with the government and to adopt a Jewish trademark. All Jews were required to declare their assets and sell their businesses. They were barred from negotiating loans and real estate transactions. They were barred from practicing medicine and law, even for other Jews. All Jews had to begin carrying identity cards classifying them as Jews.

Using the assassination of a low level diplomatic secretary in Paris by a Jewish teenager as an excuse, the Nazis unleashed a state-sponsored pogrom known as *Kristallnacht* (*night of broken glass*). Under the leadership of the SS, synagogues throughout Germany were burned and 7,000 Jewish shops were destroyed. A 1.25-billion-mark fine was imposed on the Jews, and all Jews' insurance was confiscated by the state. Scores of Jews were murdered and thousands more were mercilessly beaten.

Following the Kristallnacht, the SS rounded up 30,000 affluent Jews and sent them to concentration camps. The Nazis confiscated the wealth of these Jews and gave them permits to leave Germany. Jews were banned from schools, universities, theaters, concert halls, museums, sports stadiums and swimming pools. Drivers' licenses were suspended and all gold and silver objects except wedding rings had to be surrendered.

1939

The SS began to expedite the emigration of all Jews and the expropriation of their property. In 1939, 78,000 Jews left Berlin in contrast to 40,000 who emigrated in 1938.

In an irony of history, the Zionist Immigration Bureau in the Palestine Mandate territory and the Nazis developed a working relationship in order to help Jews immigrate to Palestine. Many Nazis opposed any cooperation with the Zionists on the basis that it would help build a Jewish state. Despite this opposition, Zionist cooperation enabled thousands of Jews to escape in 1939. This ended with the outbreak of WW II.

The Einsatzgruppen (Mobile Killing Squads) were created. They followed the conquering army and began to systematically slaughter the Jews as they were discovered. The massive relocation of Jews in Poland began as the Einsatzgruppen rounded up Jews in rural areas and concentrated them in larger towns with good railway facilities for efficient transport to death camps. The Einsatzgruppen also confiscated Jewish property and closed all Jewish organizations. They were also entrusted with the duty of destroying all groups in occupied countries that were hostile to the Reich.

The Nazis discovered that machine gunning the Jews was inefficient and having negative psychological effects on the troops doing the killing. Another solution had to be found.

1940

The Nazis created Jewish ghettos throughout occupied Poland. All Jews were to be handed over to the SS to be worked to death or exterminated. Concentration camps were established in various places. The Jewish population suffered all of the following, one after another, in sequence: economic and social discrimination, persecution, beatings, mass arrests, deportation and death. The first contingent of more than 1,000 Polish Jews arrived at Buchenwald. After 5 months only 300 were still alive.

In Nazi occupied France, orders were given for all Jews to be arrested and sent to concentration camps. The first Anti-Jewish decrees were established outside Germany in Nazi occupied Belgium.

The Chelmno extermination camp was established in Poland. Jews brought there were gassed in special mobile gas chambers using carbon monoxide. The bodies were buried in mass graves in the nearby woods. The SS made powder out of the bones of their victims which was then used in construction of walls in a nearby village. By 1944, **152,000** had been murdered by this method at this camp.

1941

Himmler's records state that in 1941, **130,000** Jews were murdered in Lithuania and Latvia.

PART 2 – AN OUTLINE OF THE HISTORY OF "CHRISTIAN" ANTI-SEMITISM

In Bucharest, the Jewish quarter and 7 synagogues were destroyed. Some of the victims were slaughtered like animals and the headless corpses were stamped *fit for human consumption*. Four hundred Dutch Jews were murdered in the Mauthausen concentration camp in Austria. Five thousand Viennese Jews were deported to camps in Poland.

Hitler issued his secret decree that Jews in occupied areas of Russia should be exterminated. He ordered that all Jews and Communist officials among Soviet prisoners of war were to be executed. All Jews living in Berlin were issued ration cards stamped with a *J* to distinguish them from the rest of the population. In Buchenwald, 104 Jewish prisoners were given experimental injections of *Evipan-Natrium*. All died. Elderly, mentally ill and physically disabled Jews were murdered at euthanasia stations.

In the United States, Senator Wheeler, Congressman Rankin and aviation hero Charles A. Lindbergh accused Jews of trying to force the country into war. Lindbergh warned of the dangers growing out of Jewish ownership and influence in motion pictures, the press, radio and the government.

On September 29th all Jews in the Kiev area were rounded up and brought to the Babi Yar ravine. They were marched in groups to the edge of the ravine and machine-gunned. Children were thrown into the ravine alive. The Einsatzgruppen murdered **33,771** Jews in two days. All Jewish ghettos in occupied Russia were systematically exterminated by similar mass shootings. In Ponar, a forest just south of Vilna, more than **70,000** were murdered. By war's end, the Einsatzgruppen murdered more than 1 **MILLION** Jews in occupied areas of Russia.

At this time, Birkenau, also known as Auschwitz 2, the largest concentration and extermination camp was established. Believing they could destroy the Jewish people with impunity, the Nazis now officially

The entrance to Birkenau death camp

stopped any Jews from emigration and ordered all Jews to be deported to death camps.

The entire Jewish population of Moravia and Bohemia was transferred to the Theresienstadt concentration camp. Jews were shipped from the occupied territories to ghettos in Warsaw, Kovo, Mirsh and Riga.

1942

At the infamous Wannsee Conference, Himmler, the head of the SS, declared, **"It is the Fuhrer's wish that all occupied territories should be cleansed of Jews from West to East."** This conference officially declared that Hitler's *final solution* to the Jewish problem **was the murder of all European Jews**. The SS was ordered to make all necessary preparations in the organizational, technical and material fields to carry out the *final solution*.

Administrative responsibility for carrying out the order was assigned to **SS Col. Adolf Eichmann**. He was assigned the organization of the *transports to the East* which was a euphemism for sending the European Jews to be killed at the extermination camps in Poland: Treblinka, Sobibor and Belzec. **The American Company, IBM,** helped to facilitate the Nazi genocide through its punch card technology. (Eichmann was captured in Argentina and tried and executed in Israel on June 1, 1962).

These death camps were built for the purpose of the systematic murder of every Jewish man, woman and child in Europe. Permanent gas chambers were constructed in these camps. No selections were performed there. As the deportation trains arrived, the victims – men, women and children – were sent directly to the gas chambers. Trains carried **5,000** Jews daily from the Warsaw ghetto to the Treblinka extermination camp. The total from the Warsaw ghetto who were murdered at Treblinka was **210,322**. In total more than **1,700,000** Jews, mostly from Poland, were murdered in these three extermination camps.

PART 2 – AN OUTLINE OF THE HISTORY OF "CHRISTIAN" ANTI-SEMITISM

The SS began the vain attempt to remove the evidence of Einsatzgruppen mass murders in occupied territories. They had the task of exhuming the mass graves and burning the bodies.

1943

Himmler ordered that *the deportation of the Jews (to extermination camps) is of the first importance.*

After 33 days of fighting, the Warsaw Ghetto uprising ended. Approximately 7,000 Jews were killed in the fighting. Those who did not escape were transferred to Treblinka. In August, a revolt by the prisoners of Treblinka caused its closing. In its brief existence of slightly more than a year, July 23, 1942, to August, 1943, more than **850,000** Jews were murdered there.

When German troops entered Tatarsk, Russia, Jewish homes were systematically looted and burned. Every Jew in the town was hunted down. Children were killed in the streets either by bayoneting or by bashing their skulls. SS troops using clubs and pipes beat 30 to death and machine-gunned everyone else.

In October, the extermination camp at Sobibor in the Lublin district of Poland began operations. The victims were mainly from east Poland, but Jews from the USSR, Czechoslovakia, Austria, Holland and France were also sent there. Exhaust gas was the method of extermination. More than **250,000** were murdered there.

The SS began destroying evidence of mass murders in Lvov. Mass graves were dug up and bodies were burned. The large bones were crushed, and ashes and bones were run through screens to recover any gold. The ashes were then spread upon local fields. Within a 5-month period, the SS sent 110 kilograms (242 pounds) of gold to Germany.

In November and December, 12,000 corpses in mass graves in the Kaunas area were exhumed and were burned.

On November 3, more than 17,000 Jews working in labor camps in the Lublin area were herded into mass graves and machine-gunned.

Throughout 1943 and 1944, horrific "medical" experiments were carried out by SS "doctors" on prisoners at the Dachau, Buchenwald and Auschwitz concentration camps. Auschwitz is where the infamous SS doctor, Josef Mengele, performed his monstrous inhumane experiments. He escaped punishment for his crimes and died in Brazil in 1979. He will not escape the Judgment Seat of Christ!!

1944

Beginning in 1944, the Nazis began to separate out young healthy men and women arriving at the concentration and extermination camps. *Selected* by SS doctors according to their fitness to work as slave laborers, they were spared immediate extermination. All others were sent directly to the gas chambers.

Up until the spring of 1944 Treblinka, Belzec and Sobibor were the main Nazi killing centers. However in May of 1944 the deportations of the Hungarian Jews to Auschwitz/Birkenau began. In this most notorious death camp, **12,000 Jews were gassed and cremated every twenty-four hours. More than 500,000 Hungarian Jews were killed there in just 10 weeks.** Rudolf Höss, the SS commandant of Auschwitz/Birkenau, boasted of the efficiency of the poisonous gas Zyklon B (Hydrogen Cyanide). In total, **1.1 million** prisoners died in this death factory; 90 percent of them were Jewish. **Approximately 1 in 6 Jews killed in the Holocaust died there.**

1945

The defeat of Nazi Germany opened the world to the horrific results of the state-sponsored, and publicly supported, Anti-Semitism. All studies of Anti-Semitism are dwarfed by the Holocaust. The magnitude of the Nazi atrocities, all clearly attested to in so many ways, is **incomprehensible**. The Nazis showed clearly and unmistakably that Anti-Semitism, carried to its logical conclusion, means, quite simply, nothing less than extermination of the Jewish people and all things Jewish.

PART 2 – AN OUTLINE OF THE HISTORY OF "CHRISTIAN" ANTI-SEMITISM

21st Century Anti-Semitism

Anti-Semitism Continues to the Present Day

Anti-Semitic beliefs, myths and stereotypes still persist and in many places are increasing. It continues to speak the same language of prejudice and hate as it has down through the centuries. Sadly, Jewish communities around the world periodically experience various kinds of Anti-Semitic incidents. You can find information of such attacks on a year by year, and country by country, basis on various websites.

Today most Anti-Semitism is directed toward the demonization and delegitimizing of the State of Israel which is fueled by the continual Palestinian-Israeli conflict. The rise of radical Islam, whose terror attacks in various countries as an expression of Muslim intentions to rule the world, has defined their principal enemy as the *Satanic* United States and its *little Satan* partner, the *Zionist/Western Imperialistic Colony*, Israel. Towards that end, throughout the Islamic world Anti-Semitic beliefs, such as Holocaust denial or minimization and the proliferation of ancient libels, are continually proclaimed in various media outlets.

There are many people who now believe that these new expressions of Anti-Semitism present, for the first time since the Holocaust, an existential threat to the Jewish people.

Prior to the establishment of the State of Israel, the persecution of the Jews was based on the fact that the Jews were *permanent aliens*. They did not belong to the *Christian* or *Islamic* religion. They lived in various countries but always considered themselves *Jews* first. Because of this, the Jews found themselves a homeless people whose residence was always by permission. With the establishment of the State of Israel, the Jews now have a haven from persecution and a homeland by right rather than by permission.

From the inception of the State of Israel to the present day, there has been a continuous barrage of Anti-Semitic and Anti-Zionist propaganda throughout the Islamic world. The entire communications media of the Islamic world is engaged in the teaching of hatred toward Israel and the Jews. Anti-Semitic stereotypes, slanders and caricatures are widely used. School textbooks, popular fiction, the press, radio and TV constantly repeat a refrain of hatred and a call for the destruction of the State of Israel.

Palestinian Christians have developed a *Palestinian Liberation Theology* that is Replacement Theology as just one more guise. They replace the Biblical promises of God to the Jewish people and reassign them to themselves. This "theology" seeks to completely reinvent the Gospels and Jesus Himself, who then is no longer a Jew, but a Palestinian freedom fighter. Those who espouse this (thank God, not all Palestinian Christians do) have joined hands with Muslims for the ultimate purpose of destroying Israel and the Jewish people.

These "Christians" sponsor the infamous *Christ at the Checkpoint* conferences where they strategically vilify the nation of Israel for protecting itself against terror attacks and Christians who stand with Israel. Islamic terror attacks against Israelis, or even human rights violations against their own Christian brethren, are never criticized. To do so would bring violent reprisals. They present to the world a *sanitized* Islam, or as I have heard it referred to as a "cute" Islam. Beware of their political agenda. It is not to *fight religious extremism*, but is an agenda focused on undermining Christian support for the Jewish people and the nation of Israel.

Anti-Semitism can often be seen in the biased portrayal of Israel in the media. The worldwide history of Anti-Semitism appears to be forgotten in current reports of Israel and the Islamic countries. Because of this, many people do not understand what the survival of Israel means to the Jewish people. Because of the secular nature of the media and our Western culture in general, most people do not have any understanding of the Biblical and prophetic significance of the Land of Israel.

Since the establishment of the modern state of Israel in 1948 out of the ashes of the Holocaust, this tiny nation has suffered constant terror attacks and wars. The list of these incidents is too numerous to print here. I urge you to take the time to read about them. They will help you to understand why, even today, the Jewish people are…

PART 2 – AN OUTLINE OF THE HISTORY OF "CHRISTIAN" ANTI-SEMITISM

"So Deeply Scarred."

As believers, we know that the Scriptures declare that because of the eternal prophetic purposes of God, Israel will always be a nation and will never be destroyed.[51] We also understand that God will *"Bless those who Bless Israel and Curse those who Curse Israel."*[52] There is also an additional blessing promised to those who *"Pray for the Peace of Jerusalem."*[53]

In order to obey these commands, stand with the Lord in the fulfillment of His present prophetic purposes and reap the harvest of blessings associated with them, *each one of us* must ask the Lord how we can personally stand against Anti-Semitism and support God's purposes for Israel and the Jewish people.

Amen!!

---

[51] Jeremiah 31:35-37
[52] Genesis 12:3
[53] Psalm 122:6

Resources for Further Study

Anti-Semitism

Books
A Historical Survey of Anti-Semitism, by Richard E. Gade
A History of the Jews, by Paul Johnson
A History of the Jewish People, edited by H.H. Ben-Sasson
A Legacy of Hatred: Why Christians Must Not Forget the Holocaust, by David Rausch
An Enemy of the People: Antisemitism, by James Parks
Anti-Semitism: Causes and Effects, by Paul Grosser and Edwin Halperin
History of the Jews, by Heinrich Graetz
Jewish History Atlas, by Martin Gilbert
Our Hands Are Stained With Blood, by Michael L. Brown
Standing Against Anti-Semitism, by Howard Morgan
The Anguish of the Jews, by Father Edward Flannery
The Broken Staff – Judaism through Christian Eyes, by Frank Manuel
The Conflict of the Church and the Synagogue: A Study in the Origins of Antisemitism, by James Parks
The Crucifixion of the Jews, by Franklin Littell
The History of Anti-Semitism (Volumes 1-4), by Leon Poliakov
The Teaching of Contempt: Christian Roots of Anti-Semitism, by Jules Isaac

Websites
Randy Felton, "Anti-Semitism and the Church," at: haydid.org
Bob Michael, "Jews as Serfs," at: uni-heidelberg.de
Max Solbrekken, "The Jews & Jesus: Mistreatment of Jews: Christian Shame," at: mswm.org
Fritz B. Voll, "A Short Review of a Troubled History," at: jcrelations.com
Classical and Christian Anti-Semitism, at: virtualjerusalem.co.il
The Simon Wiesenthal Center: motlc.wiesenthal.com
En.wikipedia.org/wiki/History_of_antisemitism
Jewishhistory.org
Simpletoremember.com/articles/a/HistoryJewishPersecution

Holocaust Studies

Books
Approaches to Auschwitz: The Holocaust and Its Legacy, by
    Richard Rubenstein and John Roth
Auschwitz – The Nazis and the "Final Solution," by Laurence Rees
History of the Holocaust, A Handbook and Dictionary, by Abraham
    and Hershel Edelheit
Holocaust Theology, A Reader edited by Dan Cohn-Sherbok
IBM and the Holocaust, by Edwin Black
Nazi Germany and the Jews, by Saul Friedlander
The Years of Extermination by Saul Friedlander
The Abandonment of the Jews: America and the Holocaust, by
    David Wyman
While Six Million Died, A Chronicle of American Apathy, by
    Arthur Morse
Witness to the Holocaust, by Michael Berenbaum

Websites
Israel's National Holocaust Memorial: yadvashem.org
United States Holocaust Memorial Museum: ushmm.org
Jewishvirtuallibrary.org
Remember.org